FISHING WITH FLOAT AND FLY

FISHING WITH FLOAT AND FLY

WILLIAM CHILD

With line drawings in the text
and jacket design by
DAVID CARL FORBES
and photographs by
BILL HOWES

FREDERICK WARNE & CO. LTD.
LONDON · NEW YORK

© FREDERICK WARNE & CO LTD
LONDON · ENGLAND

1966
REPRINTED 1970

For
SIMON
the youngest Child

LIBRARY OF CONGRESS CATALOG
CARD NO. 66 – 15688

ISBN 0 7232 0209 5

Printed in Great Britain by
Cox & Wyman Ltd., London,
Reading and Fakenham
1438 · 170

CONTENTS

Part One

FLOAT FISHING

Part Two

FLY FISHING

LIST OF PLATES

Part One

FLOAT FISHING

I

THE FIRST STEPS

I AM quite sure that anyone who wishes to become a first class angler should begin by acquiring the art of fishing with the float. Floats are wonderful little things, once you understand them – and the fish. That little float sitting on the surface shows you the unseen. There you are, sitting well back from the water when, suddenly, it bobs and twitches. One second you are sitting easily, relaxed – and the next, you are tense, your hand drops to your rod butt, you hold the slack line and you are faced with the problem of judging the right second to make the strike. You must not make a mistake. A split second too soon, a split second too late – and no fish!

Of course, when you go home you can tell everyone the story of the fish that got away, but this is not very satisfactory and no one will believe you. We anglers have a lot to put up with, one way and another, for, apart from the weather, we come in for a lot of teasing. I had a birthday card sent to me this year and on it were the words from 'The Angler's Prayer':

> *'Lord give to me*
> *to catch a fish*
> *so big that even*
> *I, in telling of*
> *it to my friends,*
> *shall have no need*
> *to lie.'*

I wonder if we are inclined to stretch – only a little – the size of that fish we almost landed? But no matter. We can take a bit of leg-pulling for we have something a non-angler can never enjoy. We know that strange and wonderful magic of the unseen

life in smooth waters running through green fields; the peaceful
hours interspersed with keen excitement. Let me set the scene. We
sit back, watching and waiting, on a warm summer day. Above us
the sky is blue, around us cattle graze in daisy-dotted grass or
seek the shade of spreading trees in full leaf, and bees hum about
the pink dog-roses. Perhaps a kingfisher, russet gold and dazzling
blue, skims upstream. There goes breath-taking beauty. The kingfisher, the honest fishing bird, has his own stretch of water. He
never poaches his neighbour's territory. And quite likely, standing
in shallow water, will be that long, spindle-shanked wader, the
heron. He is a fine looking chap, but I am not sure that I like
him too well. He is rather too wholesale in his fishing. Greedy
that's what he is, and crafty, too. If we watch carefully we shall see
that he always faces the sun so that his shadow falls behind him.
If his shadow fell in front of him no unsuspecting fish would swim
within the range of his shattering beak. Shadows spell danger to
any fish. Let them see a shadow, and they are off and away. Around
our float, shimmering like jewels, dragonflies dart and hover.
There are the big copper-gold ones, and the blue ones like living
sapphire. Everything is peaceful – until suddenly we have our
first bite.

There are many pleasures to be gained from fishing, but it is
important for the beginner to have the right attitude. Angling is
the 'gentle art', to be practised by the *gentle* person, doing nothing,
at any time, that could cause a fellow angler the slightest bother or
embarrassment. Also, a person who looks upon fishing as merely
catching and killing fish will never be a real angler. A real angler
looks upon the fish as one sportsman looks upon another. Certainly he wants to catch the fish, but not necessarily to kill it. Of course
it is permissible for an angler to take a fish for the 'pot' now and
again, but his real object is simply to pit his skill against the fish's
cunning – and may the best man win!

I know that it isn't easy to return a fish to the water, at first. I
suppose it is natural for us all to do a little bit of showing-off to let
people see how clever we are.

4

When I was about ten years old I was taken fishing for trout by an uncle who was an expert dry-fly fisherman. Because I was such a small boy I was allowed to fish with a worm. I remember, too, that I had a new rod with a cork butt, which had cost me fifteen shillings and sixpence – and that was a great deal of money in those days. I know it took a lot of saving.

Anyway, I saw my float bob . . . go down . . . come up . . . and then dive and fairly race away. I had caught a trout, and was I excited! My heart was beating like a trip hammer. I had never seen anything so lovely as that fish lying on the grass – red spotted with a golden belly – a perfect thing.

And then my uncle came along. 'I'll show you the right way to put it back into the water,' said he. 'It isn't big enough to keep, anyway.' He showed me, and between ourselves, I must admit I wasn't all that far from crying. I only know I wanted that fish, to show it to my mother, to everybody who might be interested. It was my fish, the best, the biggest fish that I had ever caught. I still think about that fish and I am pretty certain that if my uncle hadn't been there my trout wouldn't have been put back. So you see, I do know it isn't easy, especially when we begin. But as we grow into more experienced and better anglers, the idea of slaughtering fish just doesn't enter our heads. It is the sport we are after, nothing more.

Some anglers are said to be lucky because they very seldom fail to catch fish. Don't you believe it! Luck enters into every sport, or game, but not all the time. The truth is that the angler who is generally successful is skilled in the art, and there is no getting away from it.

When a general decides to fight a battle he has first to gather every bit of information he can get about the general and the army opposing him. He knows the strength of the opposing forces, how much artillery he has, and so on and so forth. But most important of all is that he should know the character of the general on the other side. Is that general careful, crafty, tricky, or is he one who is bold and will perhaps risk the outcome of the battle on one crashing stroke? Upon such knowledge plans are made. And to a lesser degree, games are planned accordingly. If the captain of a cricket team thinks there will be rain and then sun to dry the wicket he drops the fast bowlers and uses his spin bowlers.

When it comes to fishing, you, the angler, must pit your skill and knowledge against the fish's natural cunning. And your skill in casting a good line will not be much help to you if you do not know all about the fish and its habits, and how it thinks. Yes, 'thinks' is the word. Don't let anyone persuade you to the contrary. The fish is no fool and if it does not think as we look upon thinking, all I can say is that it must be a very good imitation; and an excellent reason for an unsuccessful angler to talk about bad luck.

To begin with, we shall consider all fish in general. Later, we shall consider each and every fish in greater detail, giving right and proper attention to its own particular peculiarities, characteristics and habits.

We know that fish lie with their heads upstream – that is, against the flow of the river. The reason for this is because they breathe by taking in water by way of the mouth and letting it flow out by way of the gills. Oxygen is extracted by the gills. If they lie with their heads downstream, the water would flow the other way, gills first, and that wouldn't do at all. You must remember that, because one day you will have to play a big fish. Once you've got its head downstream, it soon tires, and then it is quickly in the net!

We know, too, that fish are shy. And here is something else to remember; never let your shadow fall on the water. That is fatal. They have very keen sight and once they spot your shadow it is goodbye. Make sure that your coat or scarf is not blowing about in the wind. When you approach the water, keep well back and walk very, very gently. Heavy footsteps make vibrations and the fish 'feels' these in the water. But on the other hand, as long as you are out of sight you can talk to your heart's content.

Just as the most important, the most wealthy, human beings own the best houses, the best motor cars, so the biggest, the strongest fish take the best positions in the river! What are the best positions in a river? Where the current – the flow of water – brings the most food to the waiting fish with its head upstream.

Some human beings like to live in a town, some in the country, some on high ground, some in the valleys. So do fish. Some fish like to live in shoals, or schools — a sort of town life. Others live a quiet or 'country' life which is rather lonely. Then there are fish which prefer to live and feed near, or on, the surface of the water, which is much the same as people living on high ground. Fish which live on the bottom of the river are as the humans who like living in valleys.

Suppose I asked you if you would like a nice plate of curry for breakfast on a boiling summer day? You would say, 'Not likely, thank you.' I should be offering you the wrong 'bait'. On the other hand, if I suggested some cold chicken and salad for lunch on the same day, or a dish of Irish Stew on a cold winter day, you would say, 'Yes, please.' I should be offering you the right 'bait'. So when you go fishing you must put the right 'meal' on the hook and that is often governed by the weather.

Then again people have ideas about food. Some folk are vegetarians, others much prefer plenty of meat. Fish are the same. Roach, for instance, aren't all that keen on meat. They have a fancy for bread paste. But it wouldn't be much use offering a perch a bread paste bait. The perch is the boy for meat, especially a nice red wriggling worm.

I am sure that among the people you know, some are strong, some are bold and rather reckless, some careful, clever, even a little bit artful, and others shy. And fish are just the same. Some have *all* these characteristics. Just you wait until you are playing a big carp, then you will know what I mean. Not until your carp is actually lying on the grass – and a good way from the waterside – will you be able to say truthfully, 'Got him!'

Before you begin your fishing, why not prepare a record book? A cheap exercise book will do nicely, as a beginning. With the aid of a ruler you can divide each page into columns wherein you can

7

set down particulars of every day's fishing. You will need columns for the following information: the place; the date; the direction and strength of the wind; the temperature, whether cold or warm; rain or fine; the condition of the river, high or low; the number and kind of fish caught, with their weights and the bait used.

You will then have a record to which you can refer, and from which you will acquire a great deal of the information that will greatly help you on future days by the water. When you have had a bad day you will know where you have gone wrong, and, believe me, you learn from errors. And when you have fished properly, there is your record to remind you how you did it.

2

TACKLE

HAVING taken our first hesitant steps, we now face up to the fact that as we are going fishing, we need tackle. And this is where things can become very tricky indeed, because we need money!

A man who delves into the pages of fishing tackle catalogues should either be a millionaire or possessed of an iron will! These catalogues are more than tempting. There are rods for roach, rods for carp, and so on. When I look at the collection of rods I have, I dread to think of what I have spent on them and other

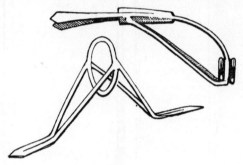

Fig. 1

tackle too. But I didn't buy them all at once. I acquired them over the years. A good rod, properly looked after, will give ages of good service. Take care of your tackle; treat it kindly. It pays.

We must have a rod. I suggest to you that we buy one that will be adequate for general float fishing. Agreed?

The rod. A three-piece, cane and a cork butt, between 11 ft. 6 in. and 12 ft. in length. There are also some glass-fibre rods on the market which are immune to almost all wear and tear. Such a rod would not be my choice – I prefer something that is more

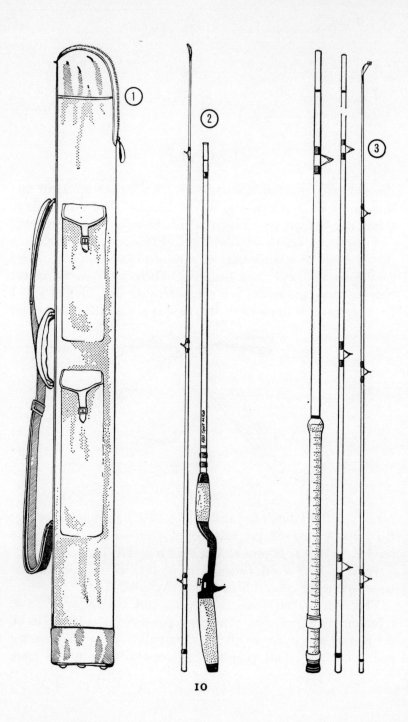

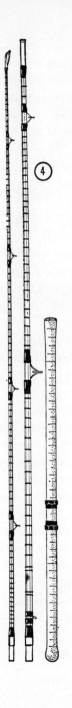

Fig. 2.   Rods for Different Aspects of Angling

1. *The rod hold-all*   A carrier for rods, protecting them from bad weather and the knocks they will encounter during a trip.

2. *The ABU Sport*   Typical of the specialized rods which are designed for spinning. Note the pistol-grip handle and the positioning of the rod rings which are designed for long effortless casting.

3. *The MILBRO Trophy*   A 12-ft. rod in tubular fibre-glass which is designed with all the action in the tip to facilitate fast striking at the slightest twitch of the float.

4. *The PETER BUTLER Specimen-hunter*   A 2-piece cane rod of 10 ft., it has an action right through, although the tip is very sensitive, and designed for large barbel, pike and carp.

'alive' – but *you* are going to use it so take your time before you make your final decision, because a rod that suits one person may not suit another. The rod that, in the words of a very wise old angler friend of mine, 'lies sweetly in the hand' is the one you should choose. Of course you must try it when the reel is affixed for without a reel the balance cannot be judged. The rings through which the line passes should be of the bridged 'stand off' type and also the first, and largest, on the bottom joint (fig. 1); the small one on the top should be 'agate' lined.

These rings play a very important part in our angling. The cheap metal 'snake rings' do your line no good at all; they will fray it and the line will snap just as you are playing a good fish to the net. The little top ring is most important; this is the one that takes the strain when the line is taut, and when your rod makes an arc as a big fish makes a last dash for weeds and freedom. 'Agate' is hard and smooth, and it doesn't crack easily.

And what is this rod going to cost? About six pounds! You could probably get one second-hand for half the price. That is up to you. But remember this: you can save up, for I think it is worth the extra money to buy a new rod. There may be anglers who have sold good rods which have no flaws, but these are hard to come by. I advise you to buy your tackle from a reputable dealer, and if possible, a craftsman. A dealer who is here today and gone to-morrow is no use to you for you will want one to whom you can turn for advice on your gear and tackle from time to time.

Very well, we've settled on your rod, reminding ourselves that we must treat it well. Never omit to dry it after a day's fishing, and a little thin oil on the metal joints keeps it in good order. Always hang your rod in its bag in a dry place. Never stand it in a corner.

The reel. The price of a reel? You can pay as much as twenty guineas for some of the very complicated kinds, but I suggest we use a nice simple centre-pin reel (fig. 3), at a price of between twenty-five and thirty shillings. It should be large in diameter and thin, so that you can wind in fast. I shall not go into the mechanical details of this reel. I think the best thing to do is to ask your dealer to give you a demonstration – which he will gladly do. You will then see how to take it apart and clean and oil it where necessary. Take good notice of how the check, or brake, works, and discover what strain, in pounds, the check puts upon the line. That really is important. If the strength of your line is up to a half-pound breaking strain, it wouldn't do for the brake to put on a strain of one pound, would it? Something would give! When we come to playing a big fish later on this will all become more apparent. Fixed-spool reels are very popular, but to begin with the centre-pin is the better choice.

We have our rod and our reel, and now our heavy expenses are

Fig. 3. CENTRE-PIN REEL

over. We can breathe again, and I shouldn't be a bit surprised if some parents aren't feeling just a little bit relieved too!

Next we need a **landing net** (fig. 4). This can be second-hand if you like. All you have to worry about is that the net hasn't rotted and that it is suitable for the water where you will be fishing. If you are fishing from a high bank you will need a long-handled job. Such a net costs about fifteen shillings. Incidentally, it isn't a bad idea to mark the handle of the net off in feet and inches. Thus, you will be able to measure the fish you catch.

Next: **lines.** Now we can get more than good value for money. When I was young it was gut and waterproofed silk, which were very expensive and needed plenty of attention. Nowadays we use nylon at about two shillings and sixpence for 50 yd. Buy yourself 100 to 150 yd. and wind it on to your reel, and there you are. We are getting along nicely now. I suggest that for general purposes we use nylon of about 1½ lb. breaking strain. It is, perhaps, a little fine, but the finer the line the less likely it is to attract the fish's attention. And it might be wise to ask your tackle dealer to recommend a brand of nylon, as some brands

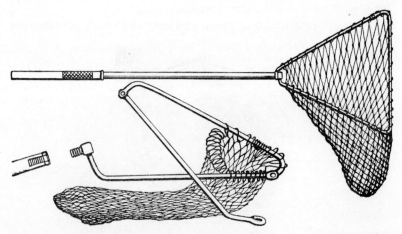

Fig. 4. LANDING NETS   Most of the available models are collapsible models, and such a net fits nicely into a tackle bag. The net is shown unscrewed from its handle and partly folded.

are not as reliable as they should be. Nylon breaking strains begin as low as a ¼ lb. One more thought. Dry your nylon – a quick rub with a rag after fishing. Nylon doesn't need the care of silk or gut, but a little care does lengthen its life.

And now: **floats.** You can make your own floats from a quill feather or a piece of cork, but these may be rather clumsy, and as those supplied by fishing manufacturers are so well made, so colourful – and cheap – I think that it is worthwhile to buy them. Colour is most important, although I must confess that my own choice of red is not very sensible. The best colours are green and yellow, particularly yellow. Yellow is the colour that shows up best on water. The decks of the Air Sea Rescue launches of the Royal Air Force are painted yellow, and also the inflatable dinghies are yellow, in order that they can be seen easily on the sea. However, you can make your own choice. Look at fig. 5. There are many other types, but these four will be enough to choose from to begin with.

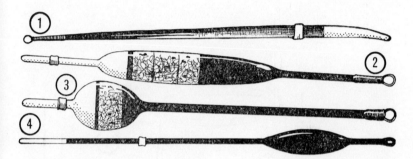

Fig. 5. SOME COMMON TYPES OF FLOAT   1. Quill.   2. Cork-bodied, for rough, fast water.   3. Grayling or Perch Bob.   4. Antennae float. Usually sunken so that only the tip is exposed for fishing in high winds.

These floats must be weighted to a degree of balance so that just a little touch will make them tell the tale of the fish having a nibble at your bait, out of sight beneath the water. If they offered even a little resistance, the fish would feel it and would become suspicious and lose all interest in the tit-bit you are so kindly offering. How is the degree of balance effected?

Split shot. Split shot is just what the name implies. For a few pence you can buy a box of these in assorted sizes. All you do is to put the line on the 'split', squeeze the shot with pincers, and the shot is fast on the line (fig. 6). You will find out by trial and error just how many you will need on your line, but don't put the bottom one closer than 1 foot to the hook. Any others should be between 4 and 6 inches apart. You will have no problems there.

Fig. 6. SPLIT SHOT

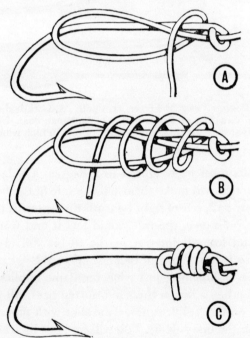

Fig. 7. TYING ON THE HOOK   A. Line is passed through the eye and laid in a bight along the shank.   B. Line is turned about both line bight and shank – at least three turns. Tucked into end of bight.   C. Reel line is pulled to close bight and draw whipping tight against the eye.

16

We still need **hooks**. Hooks are made in different sizes and you can buy them already attached to gut or nylon. But I'd much rather use 'eyed' hooks which can be bought for as little as a shilling for a dozen. If you tie the hook yourself you can be sure, having already tested your own nylon, that there isn't so much chance of a break as if you had bought the prepared job which may have deteriorated through being in stock too long, or through some other cause. The knot is very simple (see fig. 7).

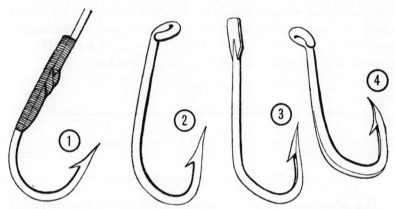

Fig. 8. FOUR COMMON TYPES OF HOOK

1. Hook to nylon – invariably in the smaller sizes, from No. 20 to No. 12.
2. *Eyed hook* Although available in small sizes, it is accepted as a much better proposition for the larger species, and ranges right up to a No. 1.
3. *Spade-end* As for the eyed hook, except that the flattened end – the spade – replaces the eye.
  In-curve A Continental hook fast becoming standard in this country. Note the eye is turned away from the line of penetration and the point turns in towards the shank.

Hooks vary in size according to the need you have of them. The sizes go by numbers, the larger the hook the smaller the number. Figure 8 shows four types. Later on, when we go fishing, I will give you the number – the size of the hook best suited to the fish we are after.

A word of caution about those hooks. Do keep them in a box which has a tight lid. If they fall out and get loose in your haversack and you happen to get one in your finger it can be very unpleasant. Don't try pulling it out. Take it along to a doctor who will do the job better than you. Still, it is better to be careful.

Next: **the disgorger.** This is a simple tool to take the hook from the mouth of a newly caught fish. It is a very simple tool (fig. 9). All you do is just push the 'U-shaped foot' down the line until it comes to the hook; a little gentle pressure, and out comes the hook and the fish is not one scrap the worse. I should have explained that whilst holding the fish, if you haven't got a wet cloth (or handkerchief) to do so, your hands must be thoroughly wet. Dry hands can do a lot of harm to a fish's scales. Do not squeeze it or you will break its internal air bladder.

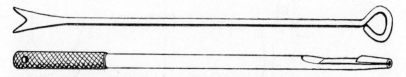

Fig. 9. DISGORGERS Two conventional models.

The plummet. This will cost only a few pence. You will need this little gadget to ascertain the depth of the water you intend to fish. I will show you how to use it in the next chapter.

Bait-tins, for maggots and worms. These tins cost only a few pennies and are so very much better than old cocoa or tobacco tins. Such old things are apt to let the bait escape in your haversack – where you will be keeping your sandwiches.

Rod rest. No cost at all! Simply cut one from the hedgerow (fig. 10). You really can't do without one. Just try sitting still for an hour or two, holding your rod. Your wrists would be more than stiff!

Haversack or **creel.** You will need some kind of container for all your tackle and your sandwiches. You can choose either a haversack or creel. I like the old-fashioned basket-work creel, but you can buy a haversack at any army surplus stores at very little cost.

I think that about covers everything you require for your fishing. You will have a pocket knife; for scissors – well, ask Mother!

Fig. 10. ROD REST

I will give you a useful tip. Tie a piece of red flannel to your disgorger, your knife, scissors, even your landing net handle. This saves time in looking for gadgets which are inconspicuous amongst the grass.

Perhaps I should have mentioned the **keepnet** (fig. 11). I don't think you need one yet; in fact I never use them at all.

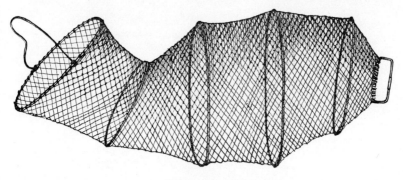

Fig. 11. KEEPNET

Once I've taken my fish, back it goes. But if you wish to keep the fish alive until you go home, you need a keepnet. And if you are angling in some match or competition or other, the net is essential; your catch must be kept for the 'weigh in'. The net is placed in the river with the open end close to your feet. Catch your fish, pop it into the open end and there it remains, alive and kicking, until you decide to let it go. A secondhand net can be had for about ten shillings, and if you feel extravagant you can spend pounds on a new one. I wouldn't!

All you need to do now is a little arithmetic and tot up just what your tackle will cost. If you are still at school, now is the time to tell your parents what a grand sport is angling, and how good and healthy, too. I will leave that part to you! Somehow I don't think you will need advice or help. I never did.

erch

pe or
iffe
lied to
rch)

Roach

PLATE 1

Rudd

ench

Common
Carp

Grayling
(normal)

Plate 2

Grayling
(Dwarf)

Grayling
(Yearling
(*above*)

Common
Bream

3

MAKING READY

WE HAVE our tackle so let us do a bit of fishing on the lawn, in the yard or in some open space close to home. Well, not exactly fishing; we'll just call it going through the motions. After all, when we go to the water we ought to know what we are doing.

We will begin by putting our tackle together.

First the rod. Fit the joints together carefully, and gently ease them into each other; and if they are a little bit stiff, a touch of grease will do the trick. Hold each joint by the metal ferrules. Never grip the cane. Cane simply hates being turned and twisted.

The rod is set up! Are the rings aligned? Good! Next fix the reel into position, firmly. There is nothing more annoying than the reel parting company with the rod when making a cast.

Next, thread the line from the reel through the rings, remembering to pull it through the top ring. Pull another 2 or 3 yd. off the reel.

Don't lay the rod on the ground. Put it up against a tree, against the wall, against anything as long as you keep it vertical. Every time I see a rod placed on the ground my heart misses a couple of beats. There is an angler's saying – and how true it is – that 'A fool lays his rod on the ground for a bigger fool to tread upon.' Don't allow your rod to be smashed so stupidly.

The float, split shot and hook are attached in that order (although when practising casting at home, it would be safer not to attach the hook).

To fix the float, just take the little collar off and slip it over the line. Now slip the line through the ring at the bottom of the float. Next, fix the collar over the top of the float, and that job is done. Test it by slipping it up and down the line. As for split shot, three will do. You know how, and where, to place them. Have you chosen a hook from the hook box? You have? Splendid! But can you remember the knot? Turn back to the sketch on page 16. It is a good idea to practise that knot until you can tie it blindfolded for there may be a time when you will want to do a bit of night fishing.

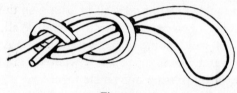

Fig. 12

There is one thing I really should have mentioned in the last chapter. Instead of fixing split shot and hook the way we have just done, you might like to prepare half a dozen nylon casts of your own. Take 1½ yd. of nylon – the length I like – and tie a loop at one end (fig. 12). Fix your split shot and tie your hook. You must, of course, tie a loop at the end of your line on the reel. Then if the loops aren't too tidy, nip the ends down with scissors, nice and close to the nylon, and join up.

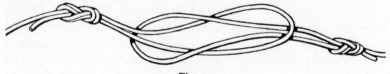

Fig. 13

The joining up is easy; look at the illustration. It is just a question of putting one loop through the other and pulling tight (fig. 13). If you adopt this method – and it does save time when you are actually fishing – you will need line wrappers. These can be cut from a piece of wood or cardboard. When you want to pack up and disconnect your tackle, push the two loops together. They will then loosen, and the rest is easy.

Now stand by for your first lesson. A little practice, a mere hour or two, and you will be casting like an experienced angler. That is worth an hour's effort, isn't it?

A good cast is accurate in direction, smooth in execution, and the bait enters the water without fuss. We will begin with the simplest way of casting. I'm all for simple methods, especially when we begin. We are able to make a good job of it and so we gain the confidence which will enable us to attempt the more ambitious and involved efforts.

Ready? But before you start, don't forget that you have a good rod. Let it do the work. Your job is to control and direct. At this stage fix a bit of cork on the point of the hook.

Begin! Hold your rod across your body, pointing to the left, about 4 ft. of your line hanging free from the top. With your left hand pull about ¾ yd. of line off the reel, holding it in four loops. These four loops are all held between thumb and finger. Now, with a movement of your wrist and forearm, bring your rod smartly upwards and across your body to the right, and then, with a final flick of the wrist, just as the top comes in line with the target – the point to which you are directing the bait – let go the loops in your left hand.

Yes, that is all there is to it.

All the same the first few shots won't be all that successful. You are bound to make a mess of them. Don't be down-hearted. Suddenly you will find that you are casting like a master.

I think it would have been as well if I had told you, straight away, that a book has certain limitations. I cannot give you practical demonstrations. Words, so often, make the simplest things seem extremely difficult. Therefore, I suggest you have a talk with one of your local angling experts. Anglers are friendly folk and I have never met one who is not willing to give a helping hand to another. If you come upon passages in this book which are not clear to you, ask him what he thinks, and, as for casting, I am certain that he will be only too happy to give you a few demonstrations and point out any small errors which you might be making.

I should like, very much, to have you using a few of the more
ambitious methods of casting, but it wouldn't help you a scrap if
I set out to describe them. By the time I had gone over the various
movements, involving the fingers of both hands, you wouldn't
know whether I was trying to teach you how to play an accordion
or tiddlywinks. It would be quite stupid of me to try. And yet
those casts are as simple as A.B.C. to understand and execute if
only you can be shown. Do make friends with, and ask the help of,
an experienced angler in your town or village. Besides, casting
isn't all that the young angler has to master.

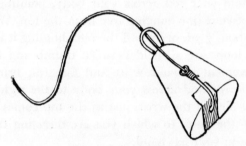

Fig. 14. THE PLUMMET

In the meantime, the simple method of casting which I have
given you is quite adequate for your immediate needs.

Now that you have finished practising the cast, have a shot at
using the plummet. Figure 14 shows how to fix it. When you go to
the water, hold your rod horizontally (taking care to keep as far
back as possible) and let the plummet down to the bottom of the
river, lake or pond, paying out line from the reel as it does so.
When it will sink no further then you have the depth. After that
you can adjust your float to the depth at which you wish to offer
your fish his dinner.

The use and purpose of the plummet is all you need to know at
the moment. We will discuss the depths at which we present our
bait to particular fish when we go after them.

I am now going to suggest that you remove your hook and float.

No, we'll keep the reel on the rod. We'll practise the strike! It is just as well to know how it is done before we have to do it.

There is nothing difficult about the strike once you've got the hang of it. I am well aware that there is a right and proper moment to make the strike, according to the way each particular fish takes the bait. Like several other things, we shall deal with the float's indication of that moment when we are fishing. Just now I want you to know how to strike. The strike in itself varies but little. You must not strike too hard or you may break the line; on the other hand you must not be too feeble, too indecisive.

Pretend your float is on the water . . . it has bobbed . . . it has dived under. . . . The moment to strike has come. Take your rod in your right hand and hold the slack line, close to the reel, firmly in your left. It won't be any use making the strike with a loose line. Strike! Now! Just a quick, firm, upward movement of the right wrist, just about three inches. There, you've done it! Try again. Keep trying until you've got it absolutely right. You must be quick, firm and decisive.

Once we have become accustomed to the strike, though we can't put it into actual practice until we have a fish on, we might as well have a talk about playing a fish. At least we shall have some idea of how to go about it.

When the strike is made the fish is hooked, and not until then shall we know, roughly, the size and strength of it. If it is so heavy and so strong – and that we must judge for ourselves – that it can break our line, it stands to reason that we must play it. The principle of playing a fish is to maintain a steady strain, never letting up, by keeping the line tight, just below its own breaking strain. If a fish is pulling at a strength of 2 lb. and your line breaks at $1\frac{1}{2}$ lb., and say the brake or check on your reel equals 1 lb. resistance, the answer is obvious. Let the fish pull on your reel. Take your hand away, hold your rod well up and let it go. An error most beginners make is that they will not keep their rods vertical. Keep it up! Once again I will remind you that you have paid good money for a good rod. Let your rod do the work for you. By holding your rod vertically, the top ring takes the strain. The top joint is sensitive; it acts as a cushion, and the pressure it puts upon the fish is constant and exhausting. You are now fighting the fish with two weapons, the pressure of the top joint, plus the strain of the line.

The fish makes its first dash upon being hooked. Let it run. Don't try to check it unless it is darting into a weed bed, or some underwater snag. Then you must risk a check in the hope of turning it; to make it change direction.

Away goes your fish. Take a quick look down to see if your landing net is close to your feet. The fish comes to the end of its first rush. Keep the strain on. Don't let the line slacken. The fish is a little bit tired. It is coming to you under the pressure. Gather the line in with your hand ... then wind any slack in with your reel. Keep the pressure on; keep your rod up.

Look out! Let go! It is off again. Away it goes! This rush isn't so far or so fast as the last. Keep that pressure on. It won't be long before the fish gets tired. As we are fishing in a flowing river – in a pond or lake it wouldn't matter – let us try to get that fish going downstream. That will tire it quickly. Do you remember what I told you earlier? A fish lies with its head upstream in order that the water can pass through its mouth and out of its gills. If it should lie the other way it would not be able to breathe properly.

So the game goes on. Gradually your fish becomes more and more exhausted until it is completely exhausted. It rolls over on its side. Bring it slowly – very slowly – towards the bank.

We will now land our fish. More played out fish have been lost through fishermen doing silly things with a landing net than will ever be known. Fishermen seldom talk of the stupid things they have done – nor does anyone else for that matter. Using the landing net properly is as simple as can be, providing it is not hurried, or we don't get over-excited.

Do not take the fish for granted, for seemingly exhausted fish often have a surprising amount of energy in reserve. I've known dozens and dozens of fish, which have looked as if they hadn't a kick left in them, suddenly come to life at the sight of the net. It is then that fish are lost. The angler makes a jab at them, using the net as if it were a tennis racket. He misses, but bangs the line, and either breaks it or succeeds in dislodging the hook from the fish's mouth. I've known a fish do a kind of half-roll, or something like a boxer's side-step, missing the net, the rim of which hit against the line, dislodging the hook . . . and there was another story of the big one that got away.

We must do the job properly. Our fish is seemingly exhausted. Your rod has been vertical. Now give it the butt! Giving a fish the butt means that you push the butt of your rod towards the fish, and that movement pushes the top of your rod backwards. At the same time, very gently, without any fuss whatever, you put your net into the water *behind* the fish. Hold it there. Keep it still. Give the fish more butt and, as you do so, *guide* that fish – there is no need to hurry – towards and over the net. Gently does it. Good! The fish is right over the net, and clear of the rim, right in the centre.

Lift! One clean, smooth hoist! The job is done; your fish is in the net. There is absolutely nothing to it at all if only you go carefully, use a bit of sense and never, never under any circumstances, allow yourself to get excited or, worse, panicky!

Move away from the water's edge and take a cloth from your haversack; put your net down, your fish still in it, and rest your rod against a tree. Soak the cloth in the water. Take the cloth and the disgorger to the net. Take the fish out of the net in the wet cloth. You don't want to harm it by using your bare warm hands. Now hold firmly, put the foot of your disgorger on your line . . . push it along until you reach the hook . . . a little persuasive pressure . . . gentle manipulation . . . and out it comes!

With both hands on the wet cloth, lift your fish and take it back to the water. Place it, still holding it firmly, under the water, head upstream. It is a very tired fish, but it won't be long before its gills are working harder. It is breathing better now so it must be growing stronger. Its fins are beginning to flutter, there's a flick of the tail. All right . . . let go!

Slowly your fish turns, and then, with another flick of the tail and the fins, it disappears from sight into the depths.

Although this has been only a rehearsal you will now be more self-assured when you start on a fishing expedition by real water, and you will see for yourself how useful the practice run in your own garden has been to you.

Before you set off for a day's fishing, check and double check your tackle: rod, reel, lines, hooks, floats, split shot, knife, scissors, disgorger, net and bait. Don't ever forget to do that.

And the final make ready? Your clothing! This is just a matter of common sense. If you fish in the winter, take two or three pull-overs as well as your normal clothing. And gum-boots, but do have the sort with barred or studded soles and heels – you don't want to slip, especially near the water. In the summer you will want to keep cool (I hope), but always take a light-weight mackintosh – one of those plastic macks will do nicely and they are very cheap too. We must always expect rain in our summers, and getting wet isn't much fun.

4

WHEN, WHERE AND PRIVILEGE

WHEN can we fish? We can fish for coarse fish only from the 16th day of June of one year until the 14th day of March the following year. The close season, three months of it, is therefore from the 15th of March to the 15th of June. And the reason for the close season, when fishing is forbidden, is because then the fish will be spawning.

However, there are one or two areas where the dates of the close season, for some reason or other, vary by a week or so. To fish during the close season is an offence – punishable too – so a young angler should, for his or her own sake, become familiar with the rules and regulations. You will, almost certainly, require a licence to fish, even on private water. This costs only a shilling or two. Your fishing-tackle dealer will know all about that and will most likely be able to provide you with your licence, subject to that small financial consideration.

Among the rules – and there will be quite a number of them – you may well find that some very popular baits are barred, especially maggots or, as some anglers call them, gentles. Maggots are usually barred on water where there are also game fish to be had, especially salmon. Two rivers I know extremely well, the Wye and Usk, are examples. The reason for this is quite sensible. Parr are salmon in their early stage of development. They have a great fondness for maggots; and because part of the close season for game fish – late autumn until early spring – coincides with the open season for coarse fish, by using maggots an angler would most probably be catching game fish when out of season. Strangely enough, worm is not banned, but the little parr will take a worm almost as readily as they will take a maggot.

I must warn you that if an angler breaks the rules and does a little poaching, not only can he be fined, but his tackle is also confiscated. The way of the transgressor is hard!

Where are we to fish? To begin with, a good angling club appears to be the answer. There are good angling clubs everywhere and they offer the angler of modest means, like you and me, first-class fishing at a very little cost; which is, of course, the reason for their existence.

Clubs buy and rent water with the proceeds acquired from members' subscriptions. Our old friend, the fishing-tackle dealer, will put you in touch with a club secretary. The secretary will then enrol you as a member of the club and give you all particulars of the club's water, and the rules. Most clubs take junior members at a reduced subscription, and usually give fishing instructions. A new member must read these rules very carefully. He may well find that certain baits are barred from use just as the Wye Water Board bars those maggots we talked about. He will discover that hempseed must not be used, according to the rules of some clubs.

All clubs lay down rules concerning the number of fish, and their minimum length or weight, that the member may take in one day. Such a rule applies only to fish which the member wishes to keep for 'the pot'. It is permissible to take a fish for 'the pot' now and again – I do myself, very occasionally, but only perch. Other coarse fish taste, to me, like cotton wool filled with pins.

What other fishing is open to the angler, apart from clubs? The best of all, if he can get it, is private fishing! As a matter of fact, it isn't all that difficult. There is any amount of it about. There are good streams and ponds on many a farm, and there is many a farmer who won't say no if asked nicely. And there are rivers, lakes and ponds on many estates where an angler can have first-class sport by buying a day ticket – just a shilling or two. There is free fishing to be had too. Such fishing usually belongs to the Town – the Town Council. I know of two such stretches of water, both in Devon, that are an angler's dream, containing salmon, sea-trout, brown trout as well as huge roach and dace. Naturally the angler has to possess a licence for salmon – four to six guineas a year – and ten shillings a year for brown trout. But there is no licence at all for roach and dace. Possibly there is a stretch of town water available to you. It is worth finding out.

How to fish? You will remember that I said, in the first chapter of this book, that angling is the gentle art and an angler must be a gentle person. An angler who flouts the rules of his club is not worth much, is he? What is more, he isn't going to be a member of the club all that long! He'll soon be flung out, and a good thing too!

When fishing, treat the water and the countryside with respect. Never leave field gates open; never break through hedgerows or walk in mowing grass. And above all, never leave litter around. Cows are inquisitive creatures and they have very odd appetites. I know of a case where a cow ate one of those polythene bags someone had left behind after a picnic. The cow died. I'll make a small bet that *that* farmer won't give an angler a day's fishing in any water on his land now. But if you behave well you will be as welcome as the flowers in May, on any water, I can assure you. There is a very real danger to birds and animals by leaving short or long strands of nylon on the bank or in the river. Many have become entangled and die a very painful death. Coil up any unwanted nylon and put it in your pocket to throw into the dustbin at home.

5

BAIT

THERE is one certain thing about angling – you may have all the tackle and gear you may wish for, but without the bait to put on the hook it won't be a scrap of good. Its importance at once justifies the care and trouble you must take in both its acquisition and preparation.

Anglers are all faddy about their baits. I have one rule which I never break. I will not touch the bait with my bare hands, just in case the fish can detect a foreign scent which they will not like. Maybe I have a tobacco smell on my fingers or a whiff of soap

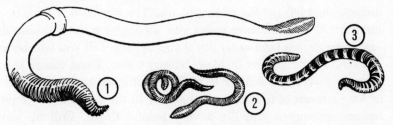

Fig. 15. WORMS 1. Lob worm. 2. Marsh worm. 3. Brandling.

lingering because I didn't dry my hands properly. So, to be on the safe side when putting the bait on the hook, I always hold it in the cloth I use for returning fish to the water.

The bait which, in my opinion, finds most favour – even with roach and dace at times – is the worm (fig. 15). To begin with, we must realize that there are different varieties of worms, and each variety has its own special appeal to the fish. One fish goes for the brandling in a big way, just as another wouldn't even look at one. We will deal with this when we set off to the river or lake.

Many fishing tackle dealers provide worms, just as they provide other baits for anglers, but if you have a garden, or you know someone who has, it is better to collect your own.

We shall begin with the lobworm, or dew-worm, and the best type of lob is the maiden, or ringless type. All lobs are worth having; the very big ones can be kept and used, when needed, as ground bait. The lob is best collected on dark nights – using a lamp or torch – after rain. Go into a field, preferably with short grass, being careful to tread lightly; like the fish, the worm feels vibrations set up by a heavy tread. Silence and speed is the secret! These lobs lie in the grass with just a little bit of their tails anchored in their holes, and with a little practice, you will be able to pick them up by the hundred.

How about keeping them? If you have a cellar at home or a dark shed put your worms in tubs or boxes which you have filled with moss, but make sure that they can't escape. The worms creep about in the moss, and scour, or clean themselves up. Keep them in this way for a few days before use; a week if you like. By the way, good moss should be collected in early summer. It should then be dried for two or three days in the sun. The moss will then last for months. Take no more than is necessary for your worm tubs or boxes, and it is advisable to cover the top with a damp sack which is much better than a wooden cover. Have a daily look at the worms, stir them around a bit, and if the moss is too dry sprinkle it with water. Any worms which are battered, bruised or dead – get rid of them. This treatment applies to all other varieties of the worm family.

Another worm is the marsh worm, and this one, I think, is the best of all. It is about 2 to 4 in. long, red in colour, and the tail is broad and flattened. The head is much darker than the rest of the body. You will find these near water, under rotting straw or vegetation, weeds or wood. Treasure them for they are a bait which takes a lot of beating.

Cockspurs you will find beneath rotting leaves, and after a day or two in the moss they become nice and pink in colour. They are small chaps, never more than 3 in. long, and they really do appeal to certain fish.

Next we have brandlings. These worms are a 'must', but they are rather smelly. You dig them out of manure heaps – old stable manure. You can't mistake them either. They have yellow bands around their bodies, and when you put them on the hook some rather nasty smelling fluid pops out of them.

I think that just about covers the worm baits, but don't forget, all worms are welcome, big and small, for those you do not use as bait come in very handy for ground baiting, of which we shall have something to say in the next chapter.

One thing about worms is that when the river is 'red', and running high and fast practically every freshwater fish will take a worm, though roach and dace must be rather particular because they don't like brandlings. Maybe they have a keener sense of smell than other fish! No doubt fish go for worms when the river is running high and fast because the worm is then a natural bait. Heavy rain which raises the river, also washes worms down from the banks. Fish know what should be expected. They are far more likely to be deceived by a bait that comes at the right and proper time.

I told you how the big fish select the best position in a river; I told you how they lie with their heads upstream just where the flow of the water brought food to them, but this applies only when the river is normal. Now remember this: when the river is fast, fish alter their positions. They don't want the effort of fighting against the power of the flow. They simply swim into the eddies and wait until the river drops. So, when the river is high and fast the eddies are the places for your worms!

In mid-summer when the ground is hard, worms are very difficult to come by. You can overcome that by keeping a little patch of your garden always wet. Cover it with wet sacking when the sun is up.

There is another way of collecting worms in the very hot weather. Take a glass – half pint size – put in half a teaspoon of mustard, and fill up with water and stir. Then go into the garden and look for the worm casts. Pour a little of your mustard and water into the hole and then stand back and keep your feet still. Remember those vibrations! After a few minutes it will happen. Pop! Up comes the worm like a cork out of a bottle. You would never believe a worm could 'pop' unless you had seen one do it.

Maggots or gentles are one of the best baits for most fish, at all times. But, as you already know, on some water they may not be used. If they are not barred in your part of the world then use them. Most fishing-tackle dealers sell them and I do think it is much better to buy than to collect them yourself. If you do wish to do so, a piece of bullock's liver is about the best method. Hang it up – where no one will be offended either by sight or smell – and leave the rest to the blue-flies. It would be as well to put the liver in, or on a piece of fine mesh wire and place beneath it a tin of bran or sawdust into which the maggots will drop.

And now we come to the wasp grub, a bait used towards the end of the summer and early autumn, and one which practically every fish will take. The wasp lays its eggs in what we call cake, a kind of tray composed of hundreds of little honeycomb-shaped compartments. The eggs become larvae – or grubs – which eventually become wasps. It is possible to buy wasp grubs from your tackle dealer. I don't advise you to try to take a wasps' nest on your own, but you can watch an expert at the job.

He will look for a little hole in the hedgerow, where wasps are flying in and out. Having located where the cake is to be found, he will wait until evening to give the wasps time to settle down. Then he will take with him a spade, a bag and some gunpowder. Gunpowder can be bought from an ironmongers. It must be made wet and kneaded into little 'torpedoes', each about 4 in. long. Your expert will clear away any obstructions to the entry of the nest. Next he will cut a turf with the spade, and light one end of one of the damp gunpowder torpedoes with a match. It will begin to sizzle and smoke. He will put it into the hole, and cover the hole with the turf, pressing it down firmly with his foot. The torpedo will give off clouds of smoke which will cloud the wasps' nest and put the wasps to sleep. As soon as the torpedo stops sizzling and smoking, he will get busy with his spade. He will dig quicky into the nest, grab the cake, brush off any wasps settling on it, and pop it into his bag. And if he is wise he will retreat hastily. Should he be unfortunate enough to be stung, wet pipe tobacco rubbed on the place will ease the pain and reduce the swelling.

Some anglers, when they return home with their wasp cake, put it in a hot oven for about five minutes. This prevents the grubs

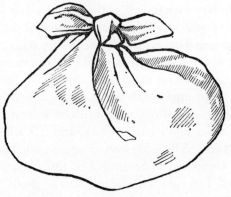

Fig. 16

from becoming wasps. Also it has the advantage of toughening the grub which is rather sloppy and difficult to fix on the hook.

And now, paste. Bread paste is most widely used of all baits and it gives the angler the opportunity to show his individuality. The normal bread paste is easy to make. Take the middle out of a three or four-day-old loaf, put it into a cloth and wrap the cloth round tightly – into a kind of bag, as shown in figure 16. Dip it in water, let it soak thoroughly and then start squeezing. Squeeze all the water out – then soak it again and squeeze some more, until the bread is like a lump of putty. This is so simple and the result is the best all round bait in use. Except the perch, grayling and, of course, the pike, paste is a favourite with all our

Pike

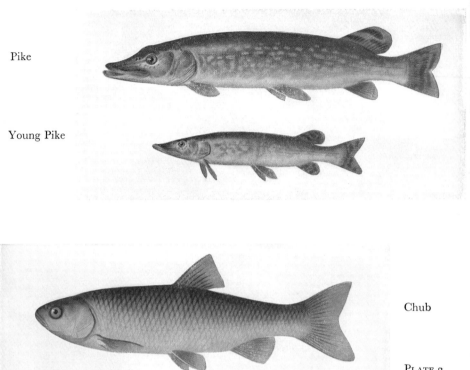

Young Pike

Chub

PLATE 3

Minnow

Dace
(*above*)

Barbel
showing
colour
variation

Trout from
moorland
stream

Common
Trout

Rainbow
Trout

Plate 4

Brook
Trout

Old male
Trout

Trout from
forest
stream
(*left*)

Young
Trout
(*right*)

freshwater fish. It has one drawback – in fast water it is apt to be washed off the hook, so your hook will need constant attention and probably re-baiting. To overcome this difficulty, many anglers mix a little cotton-wool in the bread when they make a paste. I am not sure whether adding cotton-wool is worth doing or not. I have no reason for believing that a roach, or any other fish, may feel the cotton-wool in its mouth when it takes the bait, which will make it spit it out before I can strike; yet I have a nagging suspicion that this may be so. However, try it out for yourselves.

As I said, paste gives the angler a chance to express individuality! Some believe that a little spot of honey mixed in the paste makes it quite irresistible to any sensible roach. And they may well be right. We can only judge the efficacy of a bait by the size of our catches. Then again, others swear by a paste to which cheese has been added. While I have an open mind where roach or dace are concerned, I am absolutely sure that a chub can be tempted by a bit of cheese paste.

Here is a little tip. When you are making cheese paste, use the creamy type – the kind which can be spread. This cheese mixes easily and evenly in the bread during the kneading process. The ordinary mouse-trap brand of cheese doesn't take kindly to being mixed up – in fact it is almost impossible to do anything with it. Stick to the creamy spread type and you can't go wrong.

Another fad is adding a little aniseed to the paste. You may care to try that, but be careful! It is so easy to overdo it. Enough to give the paste just the slightest scent is what you should aim at.

You'll hear about all these little tricks from brother anglers as you go along. You will probably try them all, discarding those you find to be failures and retaining those which bring success.

I know one angler – a very old friend – who mixes a little shrimp paste into bread paste and now seldom uses any other. He tells me a long story about his discovery being the result of an accident which involved a heavy storm and a shrimp paste sandwich. I have to admit that he catches some good roach on his fish paste.

So much for paste, but keep the crust of the loaf you have used. A small cube of the crust will very often tempt a fish which has lost its appetite for the more usual bait.

Now let's have a look at wheat and pearl barley. But you must be certain that both are of the best quality. Take your wheat, and soak it for at least a complete day in cold water. Then put it into a jar half full of cold water. Put that into a saucepan which has a plate laid on the bottom and is half full of water. The jar of wheat rests on the plate. I am not very good at cooking, but the idea is to prevent heat coming directly upon the jar of wheat. Put the saucepan on a gas ring. Place a cover over the jar, put the lid on the saucepan, turn on the gas and light it. Let the water simmer until the skin of the wheat bursts. Keep an eye on the 'cooking' because the wheat grains on the top generally swell and burst before the bottom grains do so. Quite a lot of anglers add a little sugar to the boiled wheat. I think the sugar is a good idea. I have had more success with sweetened wheat than unsweetened. When the wheat grains burst, the bait is cooked. Treat pearl barley in exactly the same way. Many anglers use both wheat and barley in their ground baiting. I am against it, because the grains are very filling, and when a fish has a nibble at them, his appetite vanishes. For that reason I shall omit them from the list of ground baits you will be given in the next chapter. The main purpose of ground baiting is, after all, to attract fish and give them an appetite.

And now we come to hempseed. There has been a lot said about hempseed as a bait and much written in the papers – for and against. I have no strong views either way.

To prepare the seed, soak it well for several hours; a day will do no harm. Boil it in the same way as the wheat was boiled. When the seed has burst and the kernel of the grain is exposed, then it is ready.

The way of fishing the seed is simply to drop a few grains into the water every now and again, and follow them up with a seed upon your hook. But when you strike to a bite it is usually a pure gamble and nothing else. Very seldom can the angler tell from the indications of the float just what is going on. Now and again the float does go under and then all is well – but that isn't often. And another thing – fish very quickly grow tired of hemp-seed. I believe they look upon it as a novelty when they first see it and want to know more about it, but after a while they lose interest.

Just one more bait – caddis grub or caddis worm. We will deal with the use of caddis grub as a bait later on, but when it is needed you will collect it from the water. Caddis grub is the larva of the caddis or sedge fly. You will see them crawling about in the shallows. We used to call them tram line makers when I was a

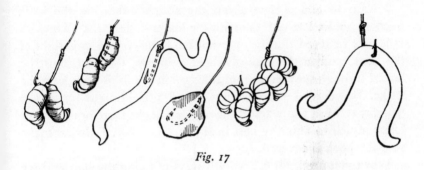

Fig. 17

small boy. The grub makes itself a little home – a stick cylinder – with its head and fore-legs sticking out. It creeps on the bottom and the stick house leaves a 'tram line' behind it. When you are by the waterside you simply collect and keep the grubs in a jar of water until needed.

There are other baits such as a cherry, a few elderberries or a small boiled potato. They are good baits at the right time. I shall tell you about them before long – and how and when to use them.

Now take a look at figure 17.

You can see how the different baits should be fixed on the hooks. If you will study, and memorize them, it will save a good deal of time when we are actually using them to fish.

There are one or two more little things I want to mention. A lively worm or maggot is far more attractive to a fish than one which hasn't any life in it. Offer the fish a bait that has a wriggle in it.

Don't forget to keep an eye on the paste baits. You must not forget that they wash off fairly easily.

If the fish don't bite, don't blame the bait. Try fishing at a different depth. If that fails, then is the time to try another bait. The watchword is patience; plus a variation of baits and depths; not forgetting that the hotter the day the nearer the surface the fish will be and the colder the deeper!

I want to add a note about the sketches showing the baits fixed on hooks. I have them with the hooks – the barbs – exposed. It is now believed that fish are not made suspicious by a sight of the hook, and in the case of wheat or hemp, the barb must be forced through the seed so that it lodges in the fish's mouth on the strike. However, I must confess that I was brought up in the belief that a fish was wary of the exposed hook; therefore I cannot bring myself to affix my bait in the modern way. I always make sure the hook is covered.

When you are fishing, try both ways of fixing the bait and see what happens.

6

GROUND BAIT

THE preparation of ground bait is, to my way of thinking, a messy, tiresome business. And for a day's fishing you need six to eight pounds of it. It isn't much good saying, 'I won't bother with it,' however much you may feel that way. You must have ground bait if you want good fishing. When you are preparing it think of the sport it will bring.

Ground bait is intended to attract the fish to the water which you are fishing; to give them an appetite for the tit-bit waiting for them on your hook.

Before we go into the preparation of the various ground baits, I would like you to remember this because it is rather important.

When we ground bait a swim – the stretch of water we are fishing in a river – we do our ground baiting at the time we are fishing. If we did it the day before, the current would, in that time, have washed our ground bait away. But when we ground bait still water, lakes or ponds, we ground bait the day before we fish. And we do so rather more generously. In still water the ground bait will not be washed away. There is also another reason. Fish are more apt to stay put in a river, but in still water they have to swim around to find food. Give them a good measure of ground bait the day before and they will be waiting for you. Of course, when you are actually fishing in still water you may give them yet another small measure of ground bait for luck.

Let's have a look at the different ground baits. For general use without a doubt, there is nothing to beat cloud ground bait. Take an ordinary white loaf, and it doesn't matter how stale it is providing it is not mouldy, and remove the crust. Then cut the white – or crumb part – into thin slices and put them into an oven. Dry them but do not allow them to burn brown. When they are nice and crisp, break them into small pieces. Then grind, or crush, the small pieces – a flat iron is just the tool for that job – and finally roll them with a rolling pin to reduce the lot to a fine powder.

Next, give it a good wetting until it is possible to squeeze the mixture into small balls. You may add a little ground rice, a bit of sugar and a little milk. The additional ingredients, one or the lot, are not absolutely necessary but they may give your ground bait that little something extra. We call this White Cloud.

Another good cloud bait can be made in the same way by using the crusts as well as the white or crumb of the loaf, and this we call Golden Cloud. There is one good thing about the Golden Cloud ground bait, the fish cannot fill themselves up on it, because it is of such a fine texture.

Then again, you may vary those two ground baits by mixing them with bran.

But if you are fishing with maggots or worms, put a few of them in your ground bait but be sure they aren't too nice and lively and too attractive. Use the sickly ones. You want the good lively worms and maggots on your hook.

If you are fishing fast running water it is as well to put your ground bait into clay balls. This is not a difficult thing to do as clay isn't hard to find. If you were to simply drop the ground bait, just as you made it, into fast water it wouldn't last long.

The way of using your ground bait comes with experience. You have to drop it into the water – without a lot of commotion – up stream from the point you intend to fish so that it will be carried to that point where you wish it to break and 'cloud' by the current.

The one rule you must observe when ground baiting in flowing water is – little and often. As you sit, every now and again – say every half hour – throw in a handful, squeezed into a ball. There is nothing difficult at all in using ground bait, yet I have a feeling you are going to think, as I do, that it is a pity the preparation isn't as simple as using it. Never mind, we forget that when the floats begin to bob, twitch and dive.

7

FISHING FOR PERCH

AT LAST we are going fishing – for perch. And it is just the day for fishing too.

'When the wind is in the North then the fishes do come forth.
When the wind is in the East then the fishes bite the least.
When the wind is in the South it blows the bait in the fishes' mouth.
When the wind is in the West then the fishes bite the best!'

That is the old jingle – and very true it is too. We have a gentle south-west wind today; just enough to ruffle the surface of the water which makes it more difficult for the fish to spot us; and not too much sun. Our luck is in!

What about bait? Worms and maggots. What sort of worms? Some of each. You never know with perch. They may feel like a nice juicy brandling, or they may like a bit of fat lob steak! As anglers, it is our duty to give them what they want. Ground bait? Certainly! A few of the not-so-lively maggots and worms to go with it. We can break up the lobs. I am not much of a believer in ground bait for perch, but we'll be on the safe side. We'll take some cloud ground bait.

Let us run through the rest. Rod; reel, with 100 to 150 yd. of nylon on it. You've tested the nylon? Good! Never go fishing without testing your lines. Net; floats – a 4-in. quill for perch; hooks – I think we'll use a number 6; knife; scissors – I'm glad to see you haven't forgotten to tie a bit of red cloth on them; cloth for holding the fish, and you are going to need it when you take hold of a perch; plummet; split shot and disgorger. Yes. That seems to be about the lot but let's re-check, just to be certain.

And your own bait? Your sandwiches, I mean. We should take a

43

newspaper, not to read for we are going fishing, but when we fish with worm we stand a very good chance of catching an eel or two, and eels can be the very devil, and no mistake. They tie themselves in knots far more intricate than any angler can devise, and they do the same to your line, and everywhere they put slime. That's why we take the newspaper. When you hook an eel, lay the paper on the grass and drop your eel upon it. I think the paper must absorb the eel's slippery slime or something like that. Anyway, the eel will keep fairly quiet. Take your knife, cut through the back bone about 3 in. above the tail, and then again just below the head. The eel will probably twitch quite a bit, but don't worry, it will be quite dead. The movements are caused by the nerves working on their own.

You will then have the job of unhooking the creature! Ten to one it will be a surgical operation quite beyond the scope of the disgorger. Eels swallow very, very quickly and very deeply.

And that reminds me about snags. There is always a likelihood, especially when working near weeds, and on the bottom, of getting snagged which means that your hook becomes entangled in weed, a sunken tree or another obstruction. Please don't start pump-handling your rod. You can do a good rod an awful lot of damage that way. Be persuasive. Get your hand to the line and leave the rod alone. And if you can't free the hook, then cut the line. With nylon at two-and-sixpence for 50 yd., you can afford to lose a couple of yards, and a hook is only one pennyworth. Besides, if you make a stupid commotion you are only going to scare the fish away. Don't damage your rod whatever you do. A first class rod, with 100 yd. of line on the reel, if used with skill will catch almost any fish.

We are now ready to set off for the river, and as we walk we shall discuss our plan of campaign. We couldn't have chosen a better fish to catch as a beginning. The perch is the most likely fish to give you some sport. Despite his humped back he is a really handsome chap with his green-gold flanks, the five or six black bars on his back, the great spiked dorsal fin, the flaming red of the under fins, the golden eyes. He is a warrior fish in looks and in ways a bold fish, fearing nothing; a fighting fish who fights to the end, as game as they come. Not even the pike can scare him. It would have to be a hungry pike indeed that would risk the scathe that great spiked dorsal fin would inflict. The perch swims unhurriedly past the killer pike, his fin – banner and weapon in one – erect and flaunting.

No, the perch can't be scared. He is a grand chap.

Where shall we find him? Where best to fish? Do those black bars on his back suggest anything to you? Do they make you think of camouflage? Then why not look for him not far from weed beds? Those black bars would make him a little more difficult to spot amongst the weeds. And besides, lots of small fish shelter in weeds, and perch have a fondness for little fish!

I don't know for what reason, but perch also like to hang around stonework – bridges and culverts. Perhaps it is because they can find some protection against the flow of water, saving themselves the effort of striving against it.

Then, on the other hand, perch swim around in large shoals all over the place, hundreds of them – mostly small and they seem to be perpetually on the look out for food.

On a very hot summer day you can see the shoals, small fish with the occasional good-sized one amongst them, basking on the surface. You will be tempted to try your luck, but I shouldn't. There won't be much doing – if anything at all.

It is my belief that the big ones don't have much to do with the shoals. I think they hang around the kind of spots I've mentioned, in twos and threes, or maybe in half dozens. How big is a really big one? Not as big, I'm sorry to tell you, as is generally believed. The biggest ever, nearing 6 lb., was caught about eighty years ago. Since then there have been a few round about 4 to 5 lb. but not a lot. If ever you catch a three-pounder you would be entitled to take it to the taxidermist and have him set it up in a glass case.

I have been fishing for many, many years, and the best I have had weighed 2¾ lb.

But here is the river! Let's cut the rod rest from that hazel over there! Now then, what about this spot? See, there's a thick weed bed twenty yards downstream, and there are rushes too. Shall we give this spot a try? Then put your rod together and fix up your tackle. . . .

Leave the question of bait for the moment. You have forgotten why you have a plummet? You must have an idea of the depth, you know. Gently does it! Up she comes! About seven feet. Now try a bit farther down . . . still seven? Try nearer the weeds . . . six . . . no, not quite. Well, now we know. We'll begin fishing at a little under six feet. And we'll begin with maggots. All set? Rod rest fixed? Then cast . . . now! Not a bad cast, either! Lay your rod on the rest and we'll sit down. Now for the ground bait with a few bits of lob worm and a moribund maggot or two. I don't think it makes much difference whether you ground bait before or after you have cast your line when you are perch fishing. For roach, bream and the others you must ground bait first. Keep that in mind. With perch you can afford to relax for you will soon know when one bites, for he will take the bait with a bang, and your float will dive and disappear immediately.

Just you wait until the shoal comes round. They'll keep you busy. No rod rest then; it will be one after the other for about twenty minutes or so. Then all will be quiet for a time. Why only twenty minutes? This is about the average period of activity. I fancy it depends on the size of the shoal and the speed at which it is moving. As long as the shoal is passing you will get bites and catch perch. They will be mostly rather small, I'm afraid . . . unless you are very lucky. The small perch are the easiest fish to catch, but the really big ones – well, I'm not certain that they aren't every bit as artful as the carp. What is happening about that cloud ground bait? Had I forgotten it? Not on your life. Just you wait a while – you'll see. And if you look upstream you'll notice that something is happening! Do you see those little tiddlers

splashing on the surface, scattering all over the place? They seem
to be in a bit of a panic. Perch on the move and the tiddlers are on
the way home before they are unlucky, so keep your eye on the
float. It could be any minute now. There! Bump-bump! See it?
Ah, you've struck too soon! Take a look at the bait. Add one more
maggot. Right! Cast again. Look out! Another bite. Wait. Your
float is diving . . . down . . . under. Now STRIKE!

You've got him. Out he comes. He is only a little one – three
ounces, no more. I'll get on with the disgorger. See how I hold
him? In the cloth and away from that spiked fin. Only a little
one, I know, but it could still hurt my hand. Now rebait your
hook and cast again. You haven't any time to waste. It will be
fast and furious for a while. I'll put the little perch carefully back
in the water again. There's another bite! Ah, you missed that one.
Now another. Away it goes. Strike! Got him! You are doing fine.
Another and another. . . . Bless my soul, you are keeping me busy
getting them off the hook! Never mind, as long as you are having
fun, then so am I.

They've stopped biting? So they have! They'll come back, or
another shoal will come along soon. What about changing the
bait? A worm, a brandling might tempt them. You have adopted
my rule of not touching the bait with your bare hands. I'm sure
that is wise. Cast out. Lay your rod in the rest. We'll probably have
to wait a little now. Good sport while it lasted, wasn't it? But not
one of them was more than four ounces. How can we get a big
one? Well, we'll have a shot. Farther downstream there is a
clearing between the reeds and weeds. It is fairly deep water.
Come on, I'll carry your bag. You bring the rod and net and the
rod rest. Let's see if we can't tempt a big one.

Here we are. Just slip the plummet on . . . gently does it. Down
she goes. Up she comes! Just about six feet. Fair enough; we'll
fish at four feet. Why? Well, if we were fishing for tiddlers, we
wouldn't want to fish right on the bottom. But we aren't fishing
for tiddlers? Well I'll explain: you want a big perch, so I am
putting a little cloud bait in to attract the tiddlers. They will

come along and then, if there are any big perch around they will
be interested, because they dearly love tiddlers. Crafty, eh? Now a
bit more ground bait. Put a nice lively worm on the hook. Cast in,
put the rod on the rest and sit back.

It is happening, sooner than I thought. See the tiddlers? They've
broken surface in a real panic. With a bit of luck. . . . You've got
it! Bang-bang! goes your float. Get hold of your rod. There it
goes again . . . and away . . . diving. Strike! Oh, nice work!
You've hooked something a bit heavier this time. Keep your rod
up! Let him run. He's ended his rush. Coax him in. I'll handle the
net! I'll put it in the water and you must bring the fish over it. I
shan't do a thing until you have your perch dead centre over the
net. That's how it should be done. Hold him! Don't give him any
more line. He's tiring. Bring him in gently . . . gently. That's the
way. He's on his side, but he may have a kick still left in him. And
I'm right, he has. Hold him. He is too tired now to make more than
an attempt to dive. Now over the net . . . hold him . . . good! Up
he comes! Take him out of the net. Watch that big fin! Here's the
disgorger. Isn't he a beauty? Look at his colours. You've done
well! He's a good pound if he is an ounce. Don't put him back. I
think you are entitled to keep this chap as he is your first good one.
Take him home and have him cooked. Jolly good he'll be, too.
I'll give him a sharp tap on the back of his head with this stone.
There, that's done it. A good fish. Well done! I think that is
enough fishing for today. You haven't done at all badly. Very
few novices can say they have landed a pounder on their first day
out.

8

THE ROACH

ANOTHER day's fishing, and you are going after roach. I suppose, taking fishing all round, the roach is the most sought after fish of all, possibly because there are plenty in every kind of water: rivers, streams, lakes and ponds. What tackle do I advise? Your rod will do very nicely. Hooks? I think a number 15 for maggot and number 14 for paste, wheat and hemp, while a size larger if you are using wasp grub. As for your float – the porcupine quill.

I look upon the roach as one of the vegetarian fish, by which I mean it is not a great meat eater, like the perch. A roach will take maggot, wasp grub and occasionally a worm, though I wouldn't offer the brandling. The time for the worm, I feel sure, is when the river is running high and fast. Then look for a deep sheltered hole out of the run of the water . . . and it won't only be roach you will catch. But we'll leave that for another time.

The 'must' bait for roach is paste, and the 'must' ground bait is cloud. It would be advisable to take one or two more. Variety is the spice of life to fish. Apart from paste, use maggots, wheat, hemp and wasp grub if late in the summer. If the elderberries happen to be ripe, and *only* if elder berries happen to be over-hanging the water, you can pick a few and offer them (fig. 18). I don't believe roach will bother with elderberries unless they know what they are, and if an elder happens to be hanging over a swim it stands to reason that some of the berries will fall into the water and the roach will know all about them. This belief is not shared by everyone, but try it for yourself and see what happens.

What about the roach itself? The biggest, weighing 3 lb. 14 oz., was taken by a Mr. Penney from Molesey Reservoir in 1938. But if you get a pounder you won't be doing too badly – and anything over 2 lb. can be considered as a candidate for a glass case!

Like perch, roach go in shoals or schools, and, again like perch, the big ones want some finding and when you find them – some catching! They are timid fish – some people call them freshwater sheep, whether because they are timid or because it is said that when one roach in a school dashes off on its own all the others follow.

Fig. 18. ELDERBERRIES

The rather hesitant bite of the roach is a very different thing from the bold knock-knock-bang-bang of the perch.

The roach is a fine chap to look at and he can put up a good fight when hooked. And when you have him landed he is so silver and shining that he looks as if he has been newly polished. His bright shining red fins have earned him the name of Red Fin.

When you catch a roach and put it back in the water, please be especially careful. The roach's scales part company with the body rather more easily than those of other fish.

There isn't much sense in fishing for roach when the summer sun is high and hot. From eight until eleven in the morning, and from about six to dark in the evening are the best times. You may have a catch in the heat of the day, but the odds are against it. In summer I like to find a nice stretch of clear water gently flowing between weeds.

Let us assume that you have found your swim. Set up your tackle and take the depth with the plummet. Set your float to the depth you think best – about a foot from the bottom – and then give the roach a bit of cloud ground bait. Having done that, give them your bait on the hook. Lay your rod on the rod rest and sit down and wait. Remember the rule about ground bait? Little and often, that's it.

You will begin your fishing with paste. You have wheat, hemp, maggots and wasp grub in reserve. If the swim you have selected doesn't prove too lucky at first try fishing at different depths. Roach have no particular depth at which they like to feed. They will even feed right on the bottom. If after trying varying depths you are still unlucky then try another bait. It isn't a good idea to search for another swim too soon. We anglers have to be patient, and patience pays dividends.

When the roach begin to feed you will probably miss the first fish. The roach bite is so very very gentle ... and then the float dives at a slant rather too quickly so if the rod isn't in your hand you won't be ready for it. Try again. You have the rod in your hand. There goes the little quiver of your float, then down it goes. Strike – and you have hooked your roach, and, if you are careful, you will land it.

But sometimes this happens: your float is still, then it rises in the water. It may even fall flat on its back. What causes this?

Take a look at figure 19. A is your float as it sits in the water; B when it rises; C when it falls flat on its back.

That is a bite, and while you are wondering what is going on your float will dive and you may miss the fish. A roach has taken your bait and he lifts it, swimming upwards. By so doing he takes the weight of the split shot so that the float rises. Possibly he swims so high that he takes all the weight from the float and so it flops flat. Keep your eyes open for that kind of bite. A roach isn't the only fish to play that trick.

Perhaps you would like to try an experiment? If the day is a hot one it is likely that a shoal or school of roach may come up to the surface to bask. They will be mostly small, but there may be a few rather larger ones here and there.

Wander about until you find a shoal basking on the surface.
Keeping out of sight put the smallest float you have on your line,
a single split shot about 2 in. above the smallest hook you have,
and set your float 3 in. above the hook. You will then be fishing
practically on the surface. Next, cast your line – oh, so very gently
– so that it will swim down amongst the basking roach. Once well
in the shoal, keep it there and watch and wait.

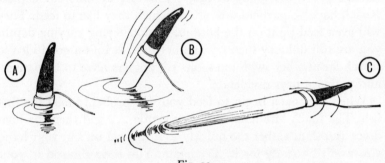

Fig. 19

If a roach does bite, the purpose of the exercise is that you will
have an opportunity to observe the way a roach takes the bait. You
would be able to see the bait and the fish, and the reaction of the
float at every stage of the take. In short – the exercise is purely
educational and well worth the effort. You can learn a great deal
from it.

Oh, and another little tip: it is a good idea to find out exactly
how many split shot each of your floats needs to be perfectly
balanced when in use. You can do that quite easily at home. A
barrel of water, a rain tub or even a bucket of water plus a little
patience will save you quite a deal of time when you are actually
on the water and fishing.

(*above*) Early beginnings

PLATE 5

(*below*) A barbel of 7 lb. which, after being weighed, is returned carefully to the water

PLATE 6   Young anglers fishing a mill pool on the River Blackwater, Braintree, Essex. A pool like this could hold a variety of fish

9

THE CHUB – OR CHAVENDER

THE CHUB or Chavender! You know, there *is* something in a name. In a way Chub suggests a rather coarse, greedy sort of creature, but Chavender – which is another name for the Chub – suggests something aristocratic, some fine heroic character from olden times.

An uncle of mine used to call that fish 'Gutsy Chub' or 'Chavender, Esquire', depending upon whether he was trying to hook one or whether he was actually trying to hold one as it made its first dart.

I don't believe there is a more greedy, 'eat anything I can get hold of' sort of fish in our rivers. Really the chub is quite a shocker. Nothing comes amiss. Paste – especially cheese paste – worms of every kind, maggots, wasp grubs, snails, slugs, caddis, elderberries, hemp, wheat, grasshoppers, flies – including butterflies – cherries, frogs and, some say, even mice are welcomed by the chub! It is said that the only thing a chub will not take is a toad. That is why my uncle called the chub 'gutsy', and I must admit that it is a very apt name.

But when he hooked a good chub and it made the first wild dash, then it earned the respectful title of Chavender Esquire! That first rush is something quite terrific. Yet once the chub has made that dart and failed to break away – it gives in. You won't find a perch, a carp or a grayling throwing in the sponge or hoisting the white flag. However, that first rush will give you a thrill. You'll have your heart in your mouth. Why does he give in? Blessed if I know, though that uncle of mine said it eats too much and so gets short of wind and stamina: something like an overweight, untrained boxer going into the ring and soon beginning to puff and blow. All the same, the chub is no fool. For the big ones you have to fish fine or you won't tempt them to take. And when fishing fine, there is the danger that in that first rush your line will be broken. On the other hand, if we use a heavy tackle then the chances are we shan't hook one.

You are free today? Good! We'll go after them and see what we can do.

Bait? Some of everything, especially a nice bit of cheese paste. And if you have cherries, white heart for preference, take the stones out. Ground bait? Just a little white cloud bait. Chub don't go in for bottom feeding, except in winter when you fish the eddies with worm. But we'll see what we can do with ground bait when we reach the water. Tackle? I think a good-sized quill not less than 3 in. Hooks? Let us use a number 7. We can't go wrong with that size.

We must find a nice stretch of water, fairly deep, fairly strong running, for the chub simply can't abide stagnation, and the bottom of the river or stream must not be muddy. There is one more essential for our stretch: it must flow beneath trees, willows and elders for preference. You will find the big ones in the shade of these trees in fairly fast clean water flowing over gravel. While the small chub aren't too difficult to catch, the big ones can cause a problem. Just one heavy footstep or a shadow on the water will put an end to your hopes of catching a good-sized one. The biggest one was caught in 1955, weighing 10 lb. 8 oz. There have been a few of 7 lb., and several six- and five-pounders, but if you catch a three-pounder you will have no cause to complain. The chub is a handsome fish with his red-tinged fins, large scales, dark brown on the back, lighter brown on the flanks and a dead white belly. But I like the build of a chub best. The hefty shoulders and tapering rounded body simply shout power and speed as you look at him.

You will put a chub back into the water without a second thought. There is no temptation to keep it for the pot. They taste like blotting paper and tin-tacks cooked in rancid margarine.

We have chosen an ideal spot, a splendid swim, so now we must be sure to have our tackle together before we go too near. Don't forget that we approach the water with more than ordinary care.

I'll take the ground bait and break it up a bit. The chub likes to be about half-way down in the water – except when the river is high and he is to be found in the eddies. He also likes to rise up to a bait. As the depth of the water under the willows here is 10ft., we shall set our float for 4 ft. 6 in. We may have to vary it as we go along. I'll drop a handful of this cloud bait in; as it is broken up it won't sink deeply and it will make the chub interested. Now put a bit of cheese-paste on your hook. In with your bait and let your line go. Follow up the ground bait as it sails downstream just beneath the surface. Keep your eyes open and be ready to strike for the chub won't waste time.

Nothing happens, so try again. But just a moment! Do you see something just below the willow, the one that is hanging almost horizontally over the water. That is a chub and a good one. It is taking something that has fallen from the tree for certain. It might be a caterpillar – in fact anything that is alive and not too big to swallow. However, we shall still try him with the paste. Bring your line in, gently with no splashing. Re-bait your hook. We're fishing fine now – our nylon is under 2 lb. breaking strain – and we will fish far. You can't beat fine and far fishing with a long line for chubbing. Cast in and let your float sail down under that tree. And don't forget – be ready to strike. Nice cast! You are coming along very well. We'll make an angler of you yet. Let your line go gently . . . another yard or two, you are almost there. . . .

You struck just a bit too soon without giving the fish time to get the paste right into his mouth. Don't give up for where there is one chub there will be others. We'll change from paste to maggots, and try again.

Gently it goes. . . . Ah, splendid! You have a good one. You've got to give line but now up with your rod and try to turn him. Hold! He's diving for the tree roots. . . .

Don't look so downhearted! You had to take a chance there. If he had got into the willow roots you would have broken your line for certain. You had a chance, if only a slight one, of turning him by holding . . . but there it is! Yes, it was a good fish – 2 lb. or thereabouts. I think it would be advisable to try another swim. We have probably scared the chub in this one. We will give them a chance to get over it and come back later. Let's have a shot in the swim over there, beyond the mill house. It looks good water to me, and the chub have shown they are not disinterested in either cheese paste or maggots. We may be lucky after all.

That little chap splashing around in the middle is a dace. Dace are gay little fish. You will soon recognize the movements of the different kinds.

Keep well back. I'll put a handful of ground bait in. There it goes! Give it time to cloud and spread around a bit. Now you can cast. Far and fine – that's the way of the good chub fisherman in summer. In winter you have to use large worms, heavy tackle and fish the sheltered holes and eddies. Look out! You have a bite! There's a piece of luck. He's darted into clear water. Give him line and let him run. Ah, his dash is over. Keep the line tight. Keep the pressure on. Rod up! You've got him! I've got the net. Bring him over it. . . . No hurry! He's coming over . . . now! Up!

And here's your chub. Hand over the wet cloth and the disgorger. You must be careful with chub. Their scales come off almost as easily as do those of the roach. The hook is out now. My word, a very nice fish indeed! A pound and a half at least. Now return him to the river. Hold him firmly in the cloth, head upstream. His gills are opening and shutting fairly easily. Let him go! That wasn't a bad effort. A pound and a half chub isn't to be sneezed at. Now let's go back to the first swim and try our luck again.

IO

DACE

Sooner or later, generally sooner, we all go after the dace. For many of us the dace, because it is so plentiful, was the first fish we ever caught – the first to provide us with the thrill of the bite and the catch. And that is an experience we never forget. We catch bigger fish as the years go by and we come to know more about the gentle art, but the memory of that first remains with us.

The dace is such a small fish; the biggest ever caught weighed only just over 1½ lb. A pounder is a giant, a half-pounder a notable fish. They generally run to only a few ounces. All the same, there isn't a gamer, pluckier little fighter in the water. The dace doesn't come in quietly. He fights to the last gasp left in him. What a pity it is that the chub hasn't the dace's heart, for, if it had, what a fight it would give the angler!

We need very fine tackle for the dace: a number 14 hook; and a small porcupine quill float, a ½-in. one would be about right. Paste is, on the whole, the best bait: a tiny piece of bread crust, maggot, wasp grub and, very occasionally, a small red worm. Will your rod be suitable? It will.

The dace is the gay fish, the happy fellow that plays in the sun. Another name for the dace is dart. That is a better name, I think, for it darts about like quicksilver. The dace is an attractive fish. Its flanks gleam like burnished silver and there is always a sheen on the blue-grey of its back.

Being a quick-moving fish, naturally enough it thrives best in fairly fast flowing water. You won't find dace in lakes or ponds. Like most fish, it is shy. It won't do for you to cast your shadow on the water, or bang your feet on the bank.

How to fish the dace? First you must know that the dace is not a bottom feeder; in fact you can apply exactly the same principles when fishing for dace as you did when you caught that good chub, even using the ground bait in the same way. But there is one difference – the strike. It has got to be *very* fast. The dace can suck the bait in and blow it out again, if it is at all doubtful or suspicious, as quickly as you can think. When your float moves off – strike! At first you will miss them one after the other, but it is good practice, and you will soon get your eye and hand in. Fish far and fine, and keep changing on your bait and depth. You will find the dace in shoals. If you go about it carefully you can take one dace after another – providing they are on the feed – from one shoal if you play your fish away from the rest. Once you've hooked one – play it away. You don't want to create a sudden alarm in the community!

Throw a piece of bread into the water. Away it sails downstream. But not for long. Up comes our little dace. He has a nibble. Up comes a pal of his; he has a nibble. Then one of *his* pals comes along and before you know what is happening there are a dozen or more all nibbling together. The bread is pushed this way and that way, and there's such a splashing of fins and tails. It is just like a game of push ball. I know the little dace like bread but I can't help thinking they enjoy the game a lot more.

You've got another question? Do dace take flies? Rather! But for the time being we are float-fishing, so we'll stick to that. Later I shall tell you all I know about fishing with the fly. However, I once used a special kind of fly-fishing with a float. And I caught chub and dace that way.

For this method you need just a small piece of cork which will be the float; cut one yourself, a little cube, say $\frac{1}{3}$ in. square. Then bore a hole through the middle and put it on your line. The hole will be too large to keep the float in one position, so push a piece of matchstick in to act as a wedge. Half an inch below the float put a single split shot. Your hook should be about $2\frac{1}{2}$ in. below the shot. Next – the bait: one dead bluebottle. Fix it on the hook, and let it swim downstream amongst the dace. Your bait will be snapped up, never fear. But, my word, the strike will have to be quick. The dace rises to the fly like lightning, splashing and flapping, and gets rid of it just as quickly, much faster than it gets rid of paste or maggot. This isn't real fly fishing, of course, but it is a jolly good way of taking dace. Incidentally, you can catch roach in the same way when they are basking on the surface in the heat of a summer day.

Good luck to you when you angle for that gay little dace, and when you catch him be very gentle with him when you put him back in the water.

II

EELS

Elvers! Elvers!

Have you ever heard that cry? What a scurry there is when someone spots the elvers coming upstream, hundreds of thousands of them. Then the people come rushing down to the river with baskets, buckets and basins to scoop up the little creatures from the water. They are young eels, fresh from the sea – little bits of things, almost transparent, and people tell me, though I've never tried them myself, that they make a very tasty 'fry up'.

The eel does an awful lot of harm to fish, for it eats the spawn which would one day become little fish and by the time it has satisfied its appetite there isn't much spawn left. Fortunately for fishermen, the otter keeps down the number of eels by feeding them to its cubs. The otter is quite an expert at catching them. And once I saw a heron with an 18-in. eel in his beak.

You would like to catch eels? That's easy enough. They haven't much sense and they are greedy. As a meal they are very nourishing, and they are particularly nice stewed, and served with parsley sauce.

Any rod will do as long as it is a good strong one. Try a number 7 hook, a fairly large float – an ordinary cork will do – and a strong line. A largish worm is the best bait, and fish at the bottom.

The best time to catch eels is after a storm – when the river is rising – or at night. But the eel isn't fussy about meal times: any time of the day or night will suit it. Don't forget to take a newspaper with you . . . and your knife! You will remember what I mentioned earlier: taking a hook from the eel can be quite a surgical operation. The more muddy the river, lake or pond, the more eels you will catch.

How big do they grow? I saw one caught on the River Torridge in Devon which weighed 3 lb. 8 oz. but the record is 8 lb. 8 oz. taken from Bitteswell Lake in 1922.

The eel is a bit of a mystery, and we don't know all that much about it. To begin with, it does not spend all its time in fresh water. It is only a lodger in our rivers and ponds, where it stays from five to ten years, and then returns to the sea where it was born.

The eel is spawned in the Sargasso Sea, the other side of the Atlantic Ocean, about three thousand miles away. Then, countless millions of the tiny thread-like creatures set out for Europe, carried by the Gulf Stream. The trip isn't accomplished in a few days; it takes about three years! And during those three years millions must have fallen as prey to fish and gulls. Then, at last they reach Europe, and up the rivers they go.

Elvers! Elvers! That is the call as soon as they are sighted in the rivers.

Once they are in the rivers the swarm breaks up. Some go up the tributaries of the many rivers, some creep out of the river and make their way across land – if the grass is damp enough – to the lakes and ponds. There they settle down. After a while the elvers become eels – brownish eels with rounded heads. For the next five to ten years they stay put, growing all the time. And one fine day they change. Their heads become pointed, their backs a shining black instead of brown and their bellies silver white. It is time for them to leave the fresh water and go back to the sea. And they do: across the fields, down the rivers – always towards the sea. Eventually they reach the sea and after that we know no more about them.

There is one thing quite certain: they never return to our rivers or ponds. For many years, naturalists have observed the eel. The big ones on the move are always travelling from fresh water towards the sea, never from the salt towards the fresh – only the elvers come from the sea.

And what happens to the eel after it has gone back to sea no one knows, and maybe no one ever will. However, what we do know is rather wonderful, don't you think?

I've no doubt the eels will give you some fun – and a lot of trouble for they are a lot easier to catch than they are to keep quiet once they are caught. Don't try landing them with a net; they make a shocking mess of the mesh. Don't stand on ceremony. Get them out of the water quickly and on to that newspaper. Good luck . . . and no tangled lines!

12

THE RUDD – AND THE GUDGEON
BY ACCIDENT

Now there's a grand looking fish for you! It looks like a roach at first glance except that it is redder and rather brighter. It is rather more thickly built than the roach. And there are two other very significant differences. Take a look at the illustration of the rudd and then at the roach on Plate 1. Do you notice anything? The dorsal fin of the rudd is nearer its tail than the roach's dorsal is to its tail. But look at their mouths: the rudd's mouth is 'pugged' or turned upwards while the mouth of the roach is turned downwards. Does that mean anything to you? It tells you the rudd doesn't feed on the bottom as the roach often does.

But what I like about the rudd is that they feed well in the hot months, July and August. Most coarse fish aren't all that eager to bite in the hot weather. Not so the rudd. It will give you good sport.

It seems a little odd to me that so few anglers know much about the rudd – or angle for it specially, as they do for roach. Maybe it is because the rudd is not found everywhere. Slow or still water with plenty of weeds is the rudd's home. There may be some good rudd water in your part of the country. If there is, go after them, especially in July or August.

How big do they grow? The record is 4 lb. 8 oz. caught in Ring Mere, Thetford in 1933. But if you get a pounder you will have done very well. Your tackle will be much the same as for roach. Your rod will do quite well. I suggest a number 9 hook. Bait? Paste, maggots, wasp grub, a small red worm – a brandling will be popular or a caddis. In the case of rudd, ground baiting is rather a problem. Rudd are surface feeders – far more so than the chub, and you recall how we ground baited for them? I think the best way to go about it is with small pieces of bread. Just break up a slice of stale bread, throw it gently into the water and wait until the rudd gather round this. They'll push it around just like a dace does. You then send your bait along and I don't think you will be disappointed.

And you can also try the little trick I use for dace: a bluebottle fished at 3 in. deep. Remember? It works very well.

How deep to angle with maggots, paste, worms and other baits? Normally anything from 18 in. to 3 ft. but you can often do very well at no more than 6 in.

A shoal of rudd makes a grand sight basking on the surface, gleaming in the sunlight. I can't recall ever seeing a rudd on its own.

Now you know a little about the rudd you can try your luck. I hope you catch them on the feed for then you will have good sport. Once you see a shoal, it is only a question of fishing fine and far, and keeping out of sight. When you hook one quickly take it clear of the shoal.

Don't waste any time in striking. There will not, usually, be any preliminary twitches. The rudd will take the bait at once; and your float will dive off sideways. Strike at once. Incidentally, if you fish no more than an inch or so deep, you will be able to observe the way the fish takes your bait as you watch the reaction of your float. We have mentioned that little trick before. It is well worth practising and, as we said, the beginner learns something.

But supposing you don't spot a shoal? Then you must look for the right kind of swim. Rudd love weed beds, water lilies and rushes. Select a swim between, or near, the weeds and slip in your ground bait. When you hook a rudd in those strips of clear water between the weeds, don't give it too much line or it will be amongst the weeds or round the lily stems, and then you can say goodbye to it. If there seems to be any danger of the rudd making for the weeds, turn it at once. You can often surprise a big one by putting on the pressure at once and turn it from its rush to safety before it realizes you have done so. Once you've got the rudd clear, or any fish for that matter, it should be yours.

Don't forget what I've told you and you will be glad you found our friend the rudd. Have a talk with your tackle dealer, or some experienced angler, and find out if they know a bit of good water. There is plenty of it in the eastern counties, and I have heard of some in Sussex where there may well be a specimen rudd, suitable for the glass case and gold lettering. But I have no doubt there are rudd to be found pretty well everywhere in England*, only one has to find the water. Yes, I'm quite sure there isn't a county in the country where rudd are not to be found, but, for some reason, while they are to be found in one pond, they will not be in water which is only a comparatively short distance away.

Would there be any gudgeon in the same water? I wondered when you'd ask me about gudgeon.

I shouldn't think you'd fish for gudgeon intentionally. You find them anywhere where there is mud, and in shallow water. They take worms, or maggots. As a 2-oz. gudgeon is quite a giant as gudgeons go – and you are more likely to pick up the odd 'ouncer' or 'half-ouncer' – I can't see any sport in fishing for them. Very little skill is needed to catch them, and you can't expect them to give you a particularly exciting fight. No, I don't think there is much point in setting out for gudgeon.

You will surely catch one or two accidentally and you won't think much of them.

*I have never heard of rudd being taken in Scotland. It is believed rudd are not to be found north of the border, but I cannot vouch for that.

13

BARBEL: THE POOR MAN'S SALMON

AND NOW you want to have a shot at the Poor Man's Salmon, do you? When I was younger we always called the barbel the Poor Man's Salmon because the barbel lives in the same fast water as salmon do, and the barbel gives as much sport, when hooked, as a salmon, and while to fish for salmon is a very expensive sport – the rent for a mile of salmon water is tremendous these days – barbel fishing is very cheap indeed.

You should go barbel fishing while you have the chance, for I have a dreadful feeling there will come a day when barbel are very few and far between. They are still plentiful in the Hampshire Avon, mainly I feel, because a very strict eye is kept on that water. But elsewhere they are becoming rare.

The reason for this scarcity is that barbel cannot exist in polluted water, and it is a sad fact that many of our rivers today are being used for disposal of rubbish, despite the laws.

Three fish share the British record at 14 lb. 6 oz., one from the Thames in 1888 and two from the Hampshire Avon in 1934 and 1937, but one half that weight will be a good catch. You will have a rare old scrap on your hands when you play him to the net. And I hope you'll do it too.

By the way, just in case you are tempted, the barbel is not a fish worth cooking. Handsome though he is, you would have to be more than hungry to enjoy a barbel cutlet.

You can never mistake a barbel for any other fish: apart from his size, he has four barbs, two each side of the mouth. And the underside of a barbel is almost flat from one end to the other. He is stream-lined. He has to be since he lives in fast water. Notice that his head is tapered to the jaw. The barbel feeds on the bottom, and the formation of the head and the general stream-lining, when pressing against the fast water, keeps the barbel's head down to enable him to find food.

In colour he varies from a rather shining brown to a darkish olive-green. The only thing I don't like about a barbel is that he has 'piggy' eyes. They spoil the look of an otherwise handsome fish.

Tackle is rather important. There is no sense in fishing too fine so you had better use a 5-lb. breaking-strain line. You'll need it if you hook a good-sized one.

Float? Cork bodied – the type we decided to use in rough water at the beginning of this book. Hooks? A number 8, I think. And be sure not to let your split shot be less than a foot away from it. That seems to cover the necessary tackle although, while you should be able to cope with your rod, if you were going to specialize in barbel fishing I'd suggest a fairly stiff rod, about 11ft. long.

We shall talk about bait and ground baiting when we've talked about the barbel himself. First we've got to keep in mind that the barbel is a bottom feeder, and then, that the barbel is a lover of fast water – the faster the better. In the early part of the season you will find that invariably they are in the shallower water, but later on they will move up into the deeper. When the cold weather arrives, the barbel isn't going to co-operate. You may get an occasional fish, but I shouldn't count on it. No, our barbel is essentially a warm weather fish – or such is my personal experience.

I suspect that the barbel is not a very shy fish, certainly not as shy as the roach and very certainly not as wary as the carp. All the same, don't forget to be cautious. There is no need to let your shadow fall on the water, or to stamp your feet about just to find out how shy the barbel really is. That sort of thing doesn't help at all.

But when it comes to knowing his water and what to do when he is hooked, there isn't a fish swimming which can give the barbel a lesson. As soon as he is hooked he makes one dash for any handy obstruction. That fish will whip round and round a submerged tree, or a rock until your line is as neat a bit of plaiting as you could wish to see. The barbel knows all the answers. If you succeed in turning him from that purpose you will still have a fight ahead of you because he doesn't know how to surrender. You can't say 'Got him' until there isn't a flick of the tail left in him.

Now we can talk about bait. You can't go wrong with paste. I have a preference for cheese paste. But as you will be fishing in fast water you will need to keep an eye on it. Paste doesn't last long in fast water. Maggots? Certainly! A nice little bunch of four or five on your hook. And a worm. Barbel have a liking for worm. The tail of a nice fat lob is often very much appreciated. Hemp, at times, will be welcomed too. The barbel is not one of the fussy fish. If one bait doesn't go – try another. But it won't be any use altering the depth more than an inch or two. You must fish on, or near the bottom. I'd say that the right depth is about six inches off the bottom, but this, again, is only a personal preference.

Ground baiting? I have a very definite notion about ground baiting for barbel. Ground bait daily for a week before you go angling for barbel. And because the water is fast, put your ground bait into clay – remember the clay balls we talked about? Bread or bran will do nicely. On the day we have chosen to fish, we give a little more ground bait, but this time we include a sample or two of the bait we are to offer. So if we are going to use maggots, we put a few of the not so lively ones in the mess of bread or bran; if it is to be worms – then a few bits and pieces. Now we'll get on with our angling. We cast – reel check off – away goes our float downstream. Let it go, for though we aren't fishing fine we'll still fish far, checking it gently over the ground baited swim. No luck? Bring the line in, cast and try again.

You strike! Just a bit too late. The float dived and up again! You must strike as the float dives. Quick is the word. The barbel doesn't play around. Now then, another try.

Splendid! Slip the check on and hold it. You struck at the right moment that time. Put on the pressure, or you'll have him playing 'ring-a-ring o' roses' round the sunken weir piles! Keep your rod

(*above*) Shepperton Weir and pool, River Thames. The weirpool swims yield roach, dace, chub, barbel, perch, and pike from sheltered swims

(*below*) A small, quiet stream needs a cautious approach. Most freshwater fish can be taken here.

PLATE 8   An early-morning tench angler in quiet and attractive surroundings

up! You've got him in clear water now and you know the form. Now let me see you play him out and then land him yourself. Good. You are going along nicely. Your fish is showing signs of tiredness. One more rush and he'll be ready for the net. Ah, here he comes. Put the net well in the water – that's the way of it. Rod up! Guide him gently over the net until he is in the centre. Lift the net up quickly. You've got him! Nice work! Four pounds, I'd say, and a very nice fish too. Isn't he a lovely olive-green? Pity he's got such little eyes. Now if he had the perch's golden eyes he'd be a real beauty!

Talking about beauties, it was while I was barbel fishing one day that I first realized what a little beauty the dipper is. You know the little diving bird which has a dark suit and a white shirt front, don't you? Things were a bit slack and I was having a quiet smoke when I spotted a dipper standing on a stone in midstream. He was bobbing up and down, never stopping. And I thought he was like a head waiter bowing to people arriving at a hotel for dinner: 'This way, Madam. A table near the orchestra, Sir?' But all at once he seemed more like the conductor of an orchestra bowing to the applause. There was the murmur of running water, the hum of insect life, the twittering of small birds, and a lark high above was singing for all his worth – an orchestra, sure enough. Now, whenever I see the little dipper, I hear the orchestra all over again, and it is very pleasant indeed. I owe that to the barbel. There is more to fishing than simply catching fish.

14

CARP

YOU have been given a day's fishing on private water – and for carp too. I can only say that I am delighted to hear of your good luck, and I hope you appreciate such good fortune. You've only been given one day, but you may wish to angle for carp again, so remember that the people who are given a day and who are invited *again* are those who behave as gentlemen. Take this piece of advice – before you begin your fishing: call upon the one who has given you the fishing, say you are grateful and then ask if there are any special private rules concerning the fish, which you are expected to observe. And while you are fishing treat the banks and surrounding land with respect, as you would your own garden at home. When you have finished the day, go to the owner, thank him again and of course tell him what sport you have had. It isn't much to do in return for a kindness granted to you.

To begin with, I suppose every angler dreams of that enormous carp he has not yet caught! And a big carp takes a lot of skill to catch. In my opinion there isn't a more artful, crafty fish in our ponds and lakes. Perhaps that is why catching one is the angler's ambition.

Recently I have heard first-class anglers saying that the carp is so difficult to catch, not because he is so clever and crafty, but because he is so stupid! Dumb is the word I've heard them called. But dumb or crafty, there can be no argument when it comes to catching the carp – they aren't easy! And when you have hooked one he fights, never letting up – pulling, pulling, pulling all the time. Oh, but he is strong and has all the courage we could wish for. You have to watch him, too, when you use the net. Just when you think he is dead centre over the net and you are going to lift –

he turns over. Up comes the net, the carp isn't there, the net rim hits the line – and that was another big one that got away!

What is the carp like? Quite handsome, but not exactly elegant. Just a little too thick-set. I am always reminded of a portly and somewhat pompous alderman, extremely respectable, eminently worthy, but too self-satisfied! Our carp is one of the same family as the barbel, but he has only two barbs (take a look at the illustration on Plate 2) whereas the barbel has four. In colour the carp is coppery, and has large scales. And how big is he? The largest recorded carp weighed 44 lb., and if you take a trip to the London Zoo Aquarium you can see the monster yourself. But don't think, for one moment, there are many carp of that weight. If I ever catch one weighing 20 lb. I shall feel inclined to buy myself a small pedestal, climb on top of it and refuse to come down. To start with you can expect to catch carp anywhere between a ¼ lb. and 4 or 5 lb. A four-pounder will give you some fun, and keep you on your toes.

They are never found in fast water. Ponds and lakes are the waters they like.

Tackle? There are rods specially designed for large carp and pike (see fig. 2) but you can make do with your present rod. You must fish fine, as fine as you dare, so the breaking-strain of your line should be about 4 lb., or 5 lb. at the most. A 3-in. quill float won't be far out. Use a number 4 hook.

Baits? Honey-sweetened paste, a small boiled potato, green peas, wasp grub, bread and worm, I think, must be your choice, though boiled wheat and hemp have their merits. The problem is when to use them. The carp is unpredictable. You must try your baits one after the other and hope you have the right bait at the right moment.

Ground baiting? Cloud, and do so for three or four days before you fish. The best way is to put a ball of ground bait in every two yards, making a path-way of it, between two likely spots from which you have selected to fish. Carp are summer fish so the times to choose are July and August especially, but after September there will be nothing doing. Some anglers are all for night fishing, but I can't make up my mind. Carp, as I have said, are quite unpredictable.

You will see bubbling, which means the carp are at the bottom of the pond, digging with their noses – probably after larvae of some description. There isn't much hope of tempting them to take your bait.

Then there are the carp which make mud rise up from the bottom – clouds of it like the vapour trails left by aircraft. These carp can be tempted and are worth trying for.

You may also tempt the carp which swims under lily leaves and sucks water snails and larvae from them. Then my trick is to cast the bait – bread or wasp grub – on to a lily leaf, wait until a carp swims by, jerk the bait softly from the leaf so that it drops naturally under the carp's nose, and hope for the best.

Carp have spasms of playfulness. They dart about the surface like a crowd of children playing a game without any rules. I once heard a story which comes from France. The French children say that frogs sit on the carps' backs and have wild races.

However, let us get down to the fishing. Your ground baiting has been done, you have chosen the positions from which you intend to fish and you are all set. If you have not done so when ground baiting – a wise procedure – you then take the depth by using your plummet. Bait your hook – and I do most strongly advise you not to use your bare hands – cast in, place your rod in the rest, sit back and wait . . . and keep quiet.

Now of all the aggravating fish, carp is the worst when it comes to biting. Your float may twitch . . . then grow still . . . and twitch again. It doesn't dive. The carp is being crafty. He is either sucking your bait off or nibbling it away. If you happen to be using paste you must keep an eye on it or you will be angling with a bare hook. The carp has a good-sized mouth so your paste offering can be as large as a walnut. Keep a watch on the bite which flattens the float on the surface of the water. Remember it? The fish lifts the bait upwards and takes the weight of the shot from the float.

Then at last comes the real bite; the one that matters. There are the preliminary twitches and then ... away goes the float and under. Whatever else you do, don't strike hard! And let the reel do the checking, all the holding, until you have an idea of the size of your fish. After that, it is up to you. You now know all the principles of playing a fish and now is the time to apply them! And if all goes well, remember the carp's little trick of turning over just as you are about to lift the net. Keep the point of your rod up and be prepared. There isn't any more I can tell you.

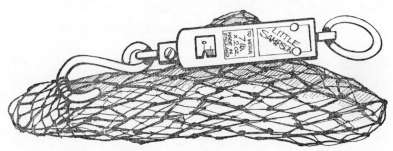

Fig. 20. WEIGHING THE CATCH   The angler weighs particularly large specimens with a spring balance in conjunction with a small net or string bag. Never put the hook of the balance into a fish's gills.

If one bait fails, of course you will try another. If you try a lob worm, use only the tail; about an inch to an inch-and-a-half of it. Be sure that the hook barb is not disclosed to the carp – whatever bait you are trying. The carp is not blind.

Would a carp make an appetizing dish? I should say definitely not, though it is considered quite a luxury by people in Eastern Europe, Poland especially. However, I understand that they use all sorts of herbs and spices in the cooking.

I once took a 5 lb. carp from a private lake at Knightwick, Worcestershire, at a time when I had come upon a recipe used by the Monks for cooking carp. I bought the herbs, white wine and all the trimmings needed, and demanded that my carp should be cooked. It certainly did not taste like any fish I have eaten, but then I don't suppose so many herbs have ever been used together before. Besides the wine, there was a lot of butter in which it had to be cooked, apart from egg-whites and bread-crumbs. As it was my fish, I ate a considerable amount, but I paid for it later and I paid for my courage. Have you ever had a bad bilious attack? They told me I looked a beautiful shade of green.

You are going after the wily carp yourself. Don't be too disappointed if things are just a little slow. But once you've landed a good one you will be as keen as mustard to catch a monster no matter how long it may take!

I5

THE BREAM

I WONDERED when you would want to know how to go about catching bream. These fish can be as aggravating as the carp in its most tantalizing mood. When fishing for bream you can expect first class sport or absolute disappointment. They either feed all out or go on a hunger strike.

There are two kinds of bream – silver and bronze. You will catch silver bream but I should say you would be angling for bronze. There are no big silver bream!

To what weight does the bream grow? The biggest ever recorded was one weighing 13 lb. 8 oz. If you catch a four pounder you can be pleased with yourself, though six pounders aren't all that rare. Of course there are the occasional eight or ten pounders, and if you take one of them it will be an opportunity for the glass case and gold lettering. I'm still waiting!

The bream is a tricky chap. When I have had a blank day fishing for bream I often think of the picture of the monks who haven't had a good day's fishing. Very doleful they look! The picture is *Tomorrow will be Friday and we've caught no fish today.*

Carp and bream were the monks' fish on Friday which was, as you know, a meatless day. I used to think to myself that they must have had a few hungry Fridays. And so they would, if they'd had to depend upon a good catch of bream or carp every Thursday! But the monks were as artful as the fish. They were always fishing and kept the fish alive in special small ponds – stew ponds – from which they could net them when needed. And they stuffed them with herbs, baked them in butter and wine. I wonder if they had bilious attacks?

I'll begin telling you about bream with a piece of sound advice.

If there is any wind from the east in the air, angle for some other fish. I have never caught any bream when there has been an east wind in evidence.

Further, I have found that winter fishing for bream is useless. Bream don't like the cold, and I can't say I blame them. Summer is the time for bream, but I will qualify that by telling you that they dislike hot sun. Before the sun gets too high in the sky and when it begins to drop in the west – those are your times. Mark you, when on a summer day there is a soft south or west wind ruffling the water, and a little cloud in the sky – that is very different!

Oh yes, you want to know about tackle. Line? Breaking-strain 3 lb., use a 3-in. quill float. Hook? A number 10 should suit. If you find a school of really big bream change over to a number 8. I'm all against very heavy tackle. After all, we aren't angling for sharks! Bait? Paste, worm, maggot. Ground bait? Bran and bread or cloud

There, now we know what we need.

Yet we must know a little more about the bream before we set off after him. He can be a very contrary chap when he likes – which is far too often for any but a keen angler. We have agreed that he is a summer fish, so we know the time of year when we are most likely to catch him. But where? In rivers and in the still waters of lakes and ponds. But bream rivers are generally slow running, with muddy bottoms, and away from the main flow there must be deep 'holes', the deeper the better, for in those holes the big ones will be found. Both in rivers and ponds there must be weed if we are to find good bream.

What more about the fish itself? The bream is, essentially, a bottom feeder. He feeds mainly upon insect life and vegetation which he collects by sucking it from the bottom. And because he is 'as deep as he is long' he has to get his tail well up to get his head well down.

Then, for no apparent reason – though some anglers believe it is preparatory to feeding – the water will become alive with bream rolling about all over the surface. Maybe they are just playing for I can't believe that they are preparing to feed. I've tried all the tricks I know to tempt them with various baits at varying depths, with never a scrap of success.

Bream travel about in schools. If you can 'get into' those schools you are in for really fast and furious sport. To do so depends on the way you use your ground bait. We will return to that matter in a few minutes.

Keep an eye open for the school travelling on the bottom. We can spot this school by the bubble trails it makes. As the school travels, the fish are poking about in the bottom mud with their noses, which makes the bubbles rise to the surface. You may have sport with this kind of school. Cast your bait in front of it. As the fish are sucking up insect life, offer them a worm. I suggest the tail of a lob. So far so good.

I now suggest that unless you know the water you are to fish, you get to know an expert angler who does, and who will point out the best places to you. It is essential that you should know the holes both in the rivers and still water. You must know where to do your ground baiting. While bream travel around in schools, they invariably return to the hole or swim. You must find two or three holes, ground bait them and stick to them. There isn't much point in wandering all over the water. You'll probably miss the schools. Use ground bait wisely and bring the bream to you.

We are getting along nicely, but just one word more about your needs. For a day's fishing I don't think 10 lb. of ground bait would be too much. You will have two or three holes or swims to feed. And one more thing: don't have your shot closer than 18 in. from your hook. Now we are all set.

You have chosen the water and you have taken the depth. Remember that the bream is a bottom feeder. I believe that it is better to fish just off the bottom – a mere inch or two. It is rather a tricky job to adjust the float correctly, but I feel it is worth it. The bream is a 'deep' fish, so while his belly is on the bottom, his nose is a few inches above. But you should try both fishing right on the bottom and an inch or two above, and learn by trial and error.

If you are fishing the river holes, I suggest you try first with paste or maggot, but if there has been rain and the river has risen, then the tail of a lob is the bait. (You may well pick up a good chub or perch with the lob tail, too.)

In still water, unless you are trying the tail of a lob in front of a travelling bottom shoal, begin with paste, and if that does not tempt your fish, try maggot. Vary your bait.

You begin to fish, and you are lucky. You have tempted a fish. But, oh dear, what a miserable little twitch the float gave! And that is the way of the bream. He is far more hesitant than the carp. He will mess about, and then – just when you are fed up – away the float will go. Then you strike. Now and again you will find that, as with the carp, your float will be 'lifted' or flattened. Of course, there will be no preliminary twitches and such like dithering. Your float will dive as if a whacking great perch had taken your bait. Keep your eyes open and keep your hand ready to strike.

I think you have all that I can tell you about bream and if you have just that bit of luck to help you to find a shoal on the feed, you will have sport, but don't be too disappointed if the day is blank. I'm sorry to tell you this, but it is no good pretending that the bream is anything like a fighter – unless you happen to hook a good one in a river hole and he gets out into the current; then you may think you've hooked a submarine!

Looking back upon my early angling days, and thinking about bream, I can see a great deal of difference in the attitude to coarse fishing. Nowadays we take fish and we put them back for another day. But in the days before the war when there were so many people without work, fish were not so often returned. This is not a fisherman's story, but I have known as many as twenty bream, weighing over 70 lb. altogether, being taken by one fisherman in East Anglia, and not one of those fish was returned! They were all for the pot. And that angler wasn't the only one.

However, what I want you to understand is not only the different attitude of the angler of today, but the sport which bream can give when they are on the feed. Twenty fish weighing more than 70 lb. altogether was not a particularly out-of-the-way catch then, nor is it today. You will have blank days. What angler does not? Yet there will be those days when the bream will give you sport you will remember as long as you live.

16

THE TENCH

THE red-eyed Doctor Fish! This is the tench. And he's worth angling for. He is as tricky as the carp, and when you have hooked a good one you will know all about it.

Why do I call him the Doctor Fish? It was supposed that sick or wounded fish rubbed themselves against the tench's slimy flanks and were promptly made well. There seems to be some truth in this claim. Only quite recently an angler living in Monmouthshire suffered from a skin disease caused by his work. He is a steel-worker. The doctor's treatment didn't work. All the ointments and lotions weren't a bit of good. Now this man caught a tench. In returning it to the water, some of the tench's slime stuck to his hands. When he went home he suddenly realized that his hands were more comfortable. He'd heard the story of the Doctor Fish so he began to wonder. He caught two or three more tench, took them home and kept them in a pond in his garden. Daily he took one out with a net, wiped his hands on the fish's flanks, put it back . . . and now his hands are as free from disease as mine are.

What does the tench look like? He is bronze-green in colour and has enormous fins and red eyes. He has two small barbs, one each side of his mouth, and he is extraordinarily smooth to the touch. How big? I have read that the record tench weighed 9 lb. 1 oz. – but a fish of 6 lb. is pretty rare. However, the tench is a strong fish – his build tells you that – and a two- or three-pounder's strength is quite surprising.

It has been recorded that tench bury themselves in the mud of ponds dried up in a drought; then they go to sleep and wait for the rain to fill the pond up again. Tench can hang on to life with precious little air to keep them alive. You can catch one, put it in wet moss, weeds or whatever is handy and suitable, and you can cart him miles to new water and he won't be a scrap the worse for the journey.

The tench, of course, is a summer fish. In the winter don't waste any time trying to catch him. He is down in the mud and weeds at the bottom of the pond having a winter sleep. Sometimes on a warm winter day a tench might take an interest in an offered bait, but it is so rare that it is not worth wasting time in trying for one.

You will find a few tench in the rivers, as you will bream, but still water is the home of the tench and in that still water there must be weeds – plenty of them.

There is a belief that tench are, in a way, governed by the breathing of the plants. You know, of course, that in the day time plants breathe in carbon dioxide and give off oxygen. When the sun has set the same plants take in oxygen and give off carbon dioxide. The tench need oxygen all the time so they hang around the water weeds while they are giving off oxygen and get away from them while they are giving off carbon dioxide. And I'm sure that this is correct. So when fishing for tench in daylight keep near the weeds; but very early morning or evening fish away from the weeds. Don't forget this, will you?

Normally the tench is a bottom feeder, but he will rise up and suck insects and snails from the underside of water lily leaves. He will also bask and roll on the surface, when you might try floating a small piece of crust.

I do wish we knew a little more about the red-eyed doctor fish. Now take the way he bubbles. The carp and the bream do so too, but the tench's bubbling is different: these bubbles are very tiny – needle bubbles, they have been called. Why so small? We know the tench is sticking his nose into the bottom mud as do the carp and bream, so why the difference in size? All we know for certain is that a tench is feeding.

There is one theory which makes sense. The tench takes some

of the mud into his mouth as he sucks up the midge larvae that he loves, and which are to be found in the bottom mud. He does a lot of chewing when separating the mud from the grub and he squirts the mud out – hence the bubbles. You can take advantage of the bubbling in the same way as we did with the bream, though I would be inclined to use a brandling rather than the tail of a lob.

Having given you something to think about, we will now have a look at ways and means.

Your rod is good enough. Line-breaking strain? Three to four pounds, and you should use a 3-in. quill float. As for bait, paste, worms and maggots are used although I prefer the worm. The trouble with paste is that the tench messes about so long, and paste doesn't stick to a hook like the impaled worm. Still, paste is a 'must' bait, so take paste. Maggots are not a must, but it is better to be on the safe side. We'll take a slice of bread in case we do a little surface fishing.

Ground bait? Bread and bran variety, a personal preference, and if it is still water you are to fish, then use the same method as we used for bream fishing.

We will angle for tench in the same way as we did for bream, only we must take even greater care in approaching the water. I am quite convinced that the tench is more wily than the bream and almost as crafty as the carp. We are up against a fish which knows all the answers. We find the depth by means of the plummet and this time we are going to fish right on the bottom. As we have not previously ground baited the hole we have chosen we shall have to be fairly generous. I think we should have a few broken worms or maggots mixed in the ground bait. After the first generous helping – providing there has been no previous baiting – the rule is 'little and often'.

In goes our bait and we sit back and hope. We may have no time to wait, or we may have a long time. All at once the float twitches. All right, sit back, don't get excited. You'll have plenty of time. The tench bite is a very long drawn out affair. There is a theory that the tench has to catch up with the bait! The tench has to feed head downwards, tail up. To keep himself in that position he has to move his fins. Remember that he has enormous fins. The fanning of those fins blows the bait away so the tench has to start all over again. Eventually he'll get a proper hold, but very often it takes quite a time. You just have to wait and be patient. Once the float goes, strike at once but be ready to hold on your check only – and also be ready to turn your fish because the odds are he will make for the weeds. And if you turn him from one bed he'll make a second dash for another. It is up to you. You can do no more than apply the principles of playing any fish which you now know as well as I do.

Remember this: tench are summer fish – June, July and August are the best months – and after September they are not worth angling for. Early morning and evening are the best times in a hot day. You may have more blank days than good days, but that doesn't mean a blank day will give you no sport. You will probably catch fish for which you are not angling. I can recall a day on private water in Lincolnshire. There had been a thunderstorm and the water had coloured. Fishing with the tail of a lob, I didn't get a touch from a tench, but I had three-and-a-half brace of bream weighing just over 24 lb. That was counted as a blank day – as regards tench. And the same thing can happen the other way round quite easily and naturally. There are very few fish which won't take worm so when baiting with worm – or maggots, for that matter – you may be angling for bream and take only tench or perch. And that will also be counted as a blank day. You know, these blank days aren't looking so bad, are they?

17

THE GREY LADY – OR THE GRAYLING

ALL fish to me are 'old chaps', except one, and she is the Lady, the Grey Lady. She is my river love, the grayling, and she is a beauty. Do you see that very small fin behind the large dorsal fin? Do you know what that signifies? It is the badge, the stamp of the fish aristocracy – the Salmon family. Yet the Grey Lady is barred from her heritage because she is born in the wrong season of the year! She is born at the same time as the roach, the carp, the bream and the rest of the coarse fish. She has always reminded me of the heroine of some Victorian melodrama, cheated of her rightful position, disdained by her family. The Grey Lady is fussy for she won't have anything but the clearest and fastest water. I've taken salmon and trout from water the Grey Lady wouldn't be seen dead in.

Hook her in August when she has got over the spawning and she'll give you a fight which the aristocratic trout cannot equal. The Grey Lady shakes the line something like a dog shaking a rat, and bores downwards at the same time. She won't give in. She has to be absolutely played out, completely exhausted, before you can steer her over the net. She is no fair weather friend. She will give you sport from the opening day of the season until the end, although, of course, she isn't at her best until she has regained her strength after spawning.

What does she look like, this Grey Lady of ours? Graceful and elegant. Her body is slim and silvery grey, dark striped and spotted, and the large dorsal fin, which rises like a sail, is barred with bluish spots. There's no doubt about it, the Grey Lady is a beauty. *Thymallus vulgaris* is the Grey Lady's Latin name because, it is said, she has a smell of wild thyme. I have heard some trout

84

PLATE 9   British waterways reservoir where there are some big carp, in addition to roach, bream, perch and tench

Young anglers fishing a popular roach swim

(*above*) This canal angler keeps well back, screened by the rushes, to ledger downstream for chub

PLATE 10

(*below*) A typical haunt of perch around the rotting wood of this old canal footbridge

anglers say they do not welcome the Grey Lady in trout water because of it. They say the wild thyme smell drives trout away. I don't believe a word of it. The rivers Test and Itchen are full of grayling, yet they also hold the biggest trout in England. On many occasions I have sniffed at a grayling immediately upon netting it and not a whiff of wild thyme could I smell.

Where shall we find the Grey Lady? All over the country, but only in fast, clear water. I believe that 5 lb. is the largest grayling recorded and I wish I could have landed her. A pounder is very common, 2 lb. is nothing to write home about, but when you take a three-pounder you will feel really pleased with yourself.

What about tackle? A lot depends upon the water you are to fish. For a high-banked river an 11-ft. rod won't be long enough, but for normal water your rod is quite adequate. I don't think I would use a larger hook than a number 8 for worm. I use a number 12 for maggot. And don't put the shot less than a foot from the hook. Float? A matter of choice, but I like a cork-bodied one – the type for rough water that we mentioned at the beginning of this book. Line? 3 lb. breaking-strain is quite strong enough.

For bait use worms and maggots in the summer and maggots in the autumn and winter. Another good bait – probably the best – is the grasshopper. Simply hook the grasshopper through the head and swim it to the feeding fish. I don't care much for using live grasshoppers, myself. Years ago, on the Teme, anglers had their own 'grasshopper'. It was made from a knot of green wool, called Berlin wool. A piece of this wool was wired to the shank of the hook and a maggot was fixed on the barb. As I haven't fished the Teme for many years I cannot say whether it still happens. It was supposed to be used on Welsh border streams too. I haven't seen it used on the Monnow which is a favourite river of mine. Anyway, you may like to try it for yourself – a bit of Berlin green wool whipped on the shank of a number 10 hook with 'hair' wire, and a live maggot on the barb. 'Make it look as much like a grasshopper as you can,' I was told. When I'd finished it looked like nothing on earth, but for some reason the Grey Lady fell for it.

We are all set to fish for the grayling. We don't want any ground bait. We have to remember that the Grey Lady does not feed on the bottom, so if the water runs at six feet, fish at three. You will have to vary the depth as you go along. The Grey Lady may be feeding only a couple of feet from the surface.

We must look for a suitable swim – fast water with gravel bottom. The best is a shallow run tumbling into deeper water. How to fish it? Swim the bait down into the deep water fairly close to the bank. Why? Because if we fished farther out and hooked a fish we'd disturb the others nearer the bank. If we have no luck with our first efforts close to the bank we can try farther out. That's sensible, isn't it?

It isn't much use fishing too long in any particular run or swim. Twenty minutes is plenty. And if we manage to take out a couple of brace, we should be content and try another run. That's one of the beauties of angling for the Grey Lady: we can wander along the river to our heart's content.

Now then, the bite. You'll have to keep your eyes open. Your bait, swimming beneath the float, will be swaying to the right, to the left, or behind or in front because it is in fast water. When the Grey Lady takes the bait it is very likely that your float will react rather oddly in a sort of sideways slip. If that happens, *STRIKE*! Don't hesitate. Of course, you will get the proper float indication as well and you already know what to do about that. Let your strike be sharp and snappy. The inside of the Grey Lady's mouth is hard, a bony structure, and if the strike is not sharp the hook will not be driven home. But don't forget that the grayling is a great fighter so, as the hook goes in, be ready to hold her on the reel check alone. I don't think there is a fish like her for putting up a fight. Certainly you cannot mistake it for that of any other fish.

We must now think of winter fishing when the Grey Lady is at her best. You may fish for her in the cold just as you do in the summer except I think that then you had better keep to maggots unless the river is really high, when the worm, small, red and lovely, is the best bait.

When the river is high and coloured this is the time when your powers of observation and your memory pay good dividends. Think of all those little gravel runs that were high and dry during the low water of summer. Can you remember where they were? If so, you are on the way to finding the good Grey Ladies. The runs may only be a couple of feet deep, maybe a little less. Swim your bait down these runs, and you may hook that five pounder I've been trying to catch for years and so far have not. Do grayling make good eating? I must confess it: they do! None better. A couple of half-pounders with cucumber sauce are delicious. I am often tempted to bring a brace home instead of putting them back, but I think you will realize how much I love the Grey Lady for I always put her back. To eat her would seem a poor way of showing how much I love her for her elegance and the sport she never fails to give me.

And I have an idea that you will love her too.

18

THE PIKE

You want to fish for pike? I knew you would. You have been hearing a few big pike stories, but I must warn you that many of the stories about big pike are not only true, they are pretty scaring. You need to watch your step when you land a good pike. But I will tell you all about that side of pike fishing a little later on.

To me the joy of angling for pike is that the pike is at his best in winter. I have never caught a specimen pike – my largest scaled only 26 lb. – but winter is the most likely time for the really big ones. And winter fishing has its own peculiar attraction. It is cold we know, but we can wrap up to keep warm, and there is a greater sense of quietude beside the water than at any other time. Have you ever noticed trees in the mists of late November? The leafless branches look like fairy lace-work. I'm not quite sure that the winter scene isn't more delightful than the summer. But there isn't any season when the waterside isn't delightful.

However, let's get back to the pike. I must confess that I don't like him. An old countryman friend of mine summed him up: 'Yes, 'e's a wicked old devil.' That's just about what he is, too. He is a ferocious killer, and I suspect that he doesn't always kill because he is hungry.

You have probably heard of a big pike near you that no one can catch and that it isn't safe to swim in that water. There are many lakes, ponds and rivers in which a monster pike, capable of nipping off a swimmer's foot is supposed to live. Don't take these stories too seriously. However, there is no doubt of the pike's ferocity. I have seen pike grab a swimming water vole, drag a water-hen underwater, and even wild duck have fallen prey to them. I know of one bit of water known as the Tunnel Pool, near a little place called

88

Wall Grange in the north Midlands, where it was believed lived a monster pike which once killed a terrier dog. I don't think anyone ever produced evidence to prove the matter, yet possibly a monster pike could do so.

There are authenticated stories of the pike's ferocity that are really quite extraordinary. One has always stuck in my mind. It was noticed that a swan was floating around with its head under the water, and as it continued to do so for an hour or more investigation was obviously indicated. The mystery was solved. A pike had attacked the swan, which is a formidable bird when angered, there had been a fight and the pike had grabbed the swan's head. The swan was killed, but the swan's head and neck had choked the pike.

Because of all these horrifying yet strangely fascinating tales about the pike, he has grown into a legendary fish who offers a dangerous challenge which no true angler can ignore.

The largest pike ever taken weighed 53 lb.! Now that was a monster! However, any pike above 20 lb. is a very good fish indeed. Another name for pike is jack, but it usually refers to a small fish: under 3 lb. in some districts or under 7 lb. in others.

Let us look at the illustration of the pike on Plate 3 to see if we can gather some clues on how to match him. We see a lean fish with the appearance of a killer. Look at his flat head, his jaws, his body built for speed! He has power stamped on every inch of him. Notice the eyes. They are set high in the skull, enabling him to see small fish swimming above. His colour, a sort of mottled olive green, tells us something valuable. It would make a good camouflage for him amongst the weeds, wouldn't it? So now we know that the pike lies unnoticed in the weeds waiting in ambush for some unsuspecting roach or other smaller fish.

And when the pike moves . . . he moves! One second he is lying limp and absolutely still, and the next he is off with the speed of an arrow. These short attacking rushes are incredibly fast when you take into account that they are made from a motionless position.

The pike is, to all intents and purposes, a lone fish. No schools for him! Even as things are, a pike is not above eating his fellow kind, so you can imagine the slaughter that would take place if a number lived together.

Pike are to be found in lakes, ponds, rivers – everywhere in fact. I began by telling you I didn't like the pike, but to be fair, I must tell you of one point in his favour. Providing water holds plenty of other fish, the pike does a lot of good for he takes the sickly or small fish and so, whilst satisfying his appetite and thus rendering the fit fish free from his attacks, he keeps the fish population within reasonable bounds. Without this rather ruthless curb on the population the small fish would multiply so quickly that there wouldn't be enough natural food for them. It has been proved that where pike have been cleared from water by netting, the condition of the fish intended to be made safe from the pike, has sadly deteriorated.

You still want to try your skill against the pike, but first I have some bad news for you. Whichever way you go about pike angling you must have very different tackle, for your ordinary rod won't do at all. You will need special equipment, and unless you have a little money already saved up you will either have to talk very nicely to your parents, fond aunts or uncles, or begin saving. Sorry about that, but that is how it is!

If for financial reasons you have to postpone your pike angling, you can at least read and make ready.

There are two methods for catching pike. You will hear that one of them is live baiting, so while I must tell you, roughly, what it entails, I want you to know I refuse to have anything at all to do with it.

The idea is to fix a live fish, roach or dace for preference, on a flight of hooks, cast it out and wait for the pike to come along and swallow it.

It has been said the roach or dace doesn't feel any pain. I don't believe that at all. There it is, stuck on the hooks without a chance. It sees the pike coming and it can't get away. What sort of sport is that? I like fish. They give me a lot of pleasure and for that reason

alone I'm not going to ill-treat them. What other anglers do is
their business. Now whose side are you on? Mine, I'll wager.

What is the other method? Spinning! Now there's some sense in
spinning. You require skill and it is sporting. Apart from that it is
far better for your health. You are taking exercise, walking and
casting. The cold weather won't do you any harm. You won't be
sitting still when the cold mists of winter descend upon you. The
likelihood of 'flu, colds or lumbago is very small with the spinner!

How do we go about it? Spinning is simply casting an artificial
metal bait which, when reeled in, spins – or revolves – beneath the
water and simulates the movements of a sick or wounded fish. Pike
go for wounded fish. What tackle do we need?

First, the rod. For a beginner, or indeed an experienced angler
who is to angle mainly from the bank, the ideal length of the rod is
6½ ft. And with the rod comes the reel. I suggest that you begin
with a fixed-spool reel because it is so much simpler to use than
other types of spinning reels. Quite a number of tackle manufacturers build rods especially for fixed-spool spinning. Therefore, it
is advisable to buy the rod for the job.

What will rod and reel cost? You could spend a great deal on
the reel alone, so I think in this case I'd go for a second-hand one.
If you have made friends with your tackle dealer I should be
inclined to have a chat with him. Put yourself in his hands. He
would see that the rod and reel were not faulty and I think five
pounds would see you through. The advantage of a second-hand
rod and reel is that they would be better quality than those we
could afford to buy new.

Line? 8 lb. breaking-strain about 100 to 150 yd. long. You
will need a 10-in. gag (fig. 21). This is a 'must' for pike have
teeth! And you will want a longer disgorger than the one you
already possess. It should be about a foot long. Then you will
need traces. These are of wire (fig. 22) fixed to the main line by
means of a swivel (fig. 23) to assist the bait's revolutions under
water. And weights. For our purpose they must be spiral leads
(fig. 22). Buy several of different sizes.

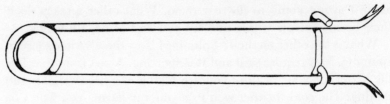

Fig. 21. THE GAG   Never put your fingers into a pike's mouth until this has been placed.

Fig. 22. THE TRACE AND SPIRAL LEAD.

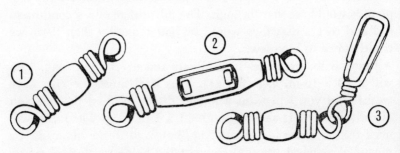

Fig. 23. SWIVELS   1. Standard swivel.   2. Box swivel, generally accepted as the strongest type available.   3. Link swivel, invaluable as a time-saver for changing traces on pike or other spinning rigs.

Now comes the moment of decision! What type of spinning bait? You are just beginning to learn the art so the answer must be the spoon bait (fig. 24).

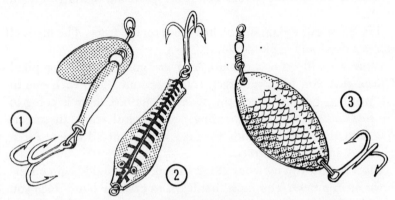

Fig. 24. TYPES OF SPOON AND PLUG   1. Gillarex Spoon.   2. Tillin Teaser. 3. Ninette Spoon.

There are various types of spinning minnows and the American plug baits. They have certain disadvantages with which I don't want to confuse you, but apart from the simplicity of the spoon, it is, in my opinion which is backed by experience, far more acceptable to the pike. So let's settle for the spoon.

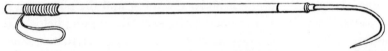

Fig. 25. THE GAFF   Whip a wrist-cord to the gaff handle to ensure a good grip during the cold weather of the pike season.

Anything else? A gaff. A gaff is only a hook on a stick (fig. 25). You can pick up one for next to nothing if you look around. But be careful with it. Keep a cork on the sharp end of the hook! You can buy gaffs which have their own protection and that is sensible. I think you are now equipped.

To set up your gear, fit the reel to the rod. Thread the line through the rings, and attach the line to the trace. See figure 31,1, on page 120, for the knot. Simple isn't it?

Fix the trace to the spoon. You can't go wrong there. Just hook it on.

Fix the spiral weight on the line – not on the trace. The method doesn't need any explanation.

Now we will do a check up. You are going to spin for pike! Check that you have rod, reel, traces, spoons (keep each one in its own box because if you put them in one box there is going to be some annoying hook tangling), gaff, spiral leads, disgorger, gag and the piece of cloth we take with us at all times. All is checked and found correct.

How should you use your gear? I think you should begin on the lawn or in a field. You must first learn to cast the bait. Once you can do that the rest is simple.

Figure 26 clearly shows the method of casting. If I wrote page after page on casting it would only serve to bewilder you – as I have said before. After an hour's practice under good guidance you should be sufficiently skilled to make your first sally against the pike. You will have no bother to discover an angler who knows his spinning to give you an hour of his time. I've taught dozens of people and have been delighted to do it.

We go to the water and now I'll tell you one thing about a spoon. It sets up vibrations under the water and the pike, even if he doesn't see the bait at once, feels them. Everything helps! I'll admit a spinning minnow does the same but not to the same degree.

Pike, we already know, lie in ambush; therefore we must spin near weeds; on the fringe of weed or rush beds.

Now we must think how a wounded fish behaves, for the spoon must behave in the same way. Its progress must not be even. It must falter, waver, make sudden little spurts, it must sink and it must rise. Got the idea? You cast out well and truly; your spoon hits the water and you begin to wind in. To obtain the wounded

fish effect, you wind in quickly, then you wind in slowly: you just
vary the speed of winding. The bait rises with speed, sinks when
slowed down. You can amplify the effect by raising or lowering
the top of your rod. Keep this in mind. If you would be a successful spinner, put all you know into making your spoon spin on
an even course of varying depth and speed in order to deceive the

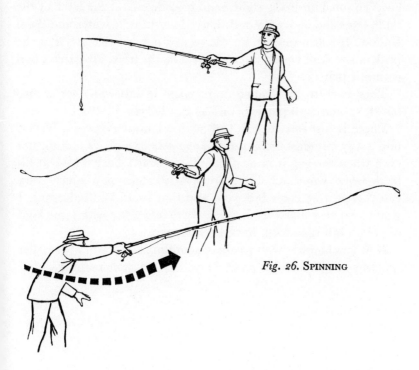

Fig. 26. SPINNING

pike. It is so very easy. What depth? You can only discover that
for yourself. It all depends upon the mood of the pike. The one
certain thing is that the colder the water the deeper the fish will
be. And the colder the day the heavier will be the spiral lead you
must use.

Let's get on with the spinning. We wander along the bank,
casting, retrieving, casting, retrieving and then – bump! We've

hooked a nice pike. Play him just as you would play any other fish, until you come to land him. Keep his head up, well out of the water. Then the gaff! Put the hook under his gills and lift. That's all. You won't do him any harm. He is on the bank. Be careful how you go about it. Stick the gag into his mouth. Then he's harmless. Out with the disgorger and remove the spoon and the gag. To put him back, right hand grips firmly at the back of the skull, left hand above the tail; lower him into the water and there he goes. If you want him for the pan or pot, a quick crack at the back of the skull with a flat stone will do the trick. Pike aren't bad eating, I believe.

They have to be cleaned and soaked in salt water for twelve hours, stuffed with parsley stuffing and baked.

There is just one little bit of advice I must give you. Never, under any circumstances, put your fingers in a pike's mouth, not even when the gag is in or if the pike is dead! Take a look at his teeth when you catch him. You can scratch your fingers very easily even if he can't bite you, and that could be unpleasant. I won't say every pike's teeth are likely to infect you with some kind of poison but such cases have been known.

Now you know how to go about spinning, and if you use smaller spoons you will take big perch in exactly the same manner.

19

LEDGERING

Now that we have had a lesson on spinning it would be unfair if we failed to mention, however briefly, the technique of ledgering, for this method can be used to fish any water under any conditions, although in my opinion it cannot be compared with the excitement and challenge of fishing with the float.

Ledgering is usually carried out in deep fast water when only a

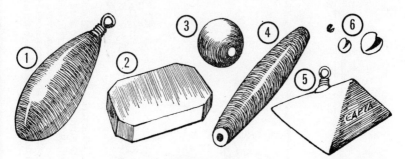

Fig. 27. ANGLING LEADS 1. Arlesey bomb. 2. Coffin lead. 3. Drilled bullet. 4. Barrel lead. 5. Capta weight. 6. Split shot – at their smallest known as dust shot, at their largest, swan shot.

heavy weight will take the bait to the bottom (fig. 27). In still-water lighter leads are used. Heavily weeded bottoms also require ledgering. Look at figure 28 to see how to set up the tackle for these different conditions.

If you have a fixed-spool reel ledgering presents no problem. With the centre-pin reel it is still possible although a little more tricky; to make a good cast with this reel pull off the amount of line necessary to take your bait to the required distance, coiling

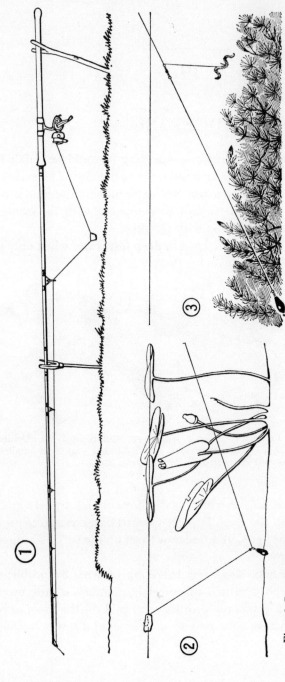

Fig. 28. LEDGERING

1. Tinfoil, or dough bobbin bite indicator for ledgering. The forward rod rest should allow a free-way for the line, and the rod should be set pointing at the water to minimize resistance to a taking fish. Generally restricted to use in still-water.

2. Arlesey bomb stopped on line by split shot, at predetermined depth, to anchor floating crust. A very effective method for carp and large rudd.

3. Ledger weight tied direct to main line with swivel and short trace to suspend bait clear of heavily weeded bottoms. Primarily for use when conditions do not lend themselves to normal float fishing. An attractive method for perch.

the line neatly on a newspaper or mackintosh spread on the ground to avoid a tangle. Make the cast with a steady swing, keeping the tip of the rod pointing in the direction of the bait. When the bait has sunk to the bottom place the rod in the rod rest, fix the bite

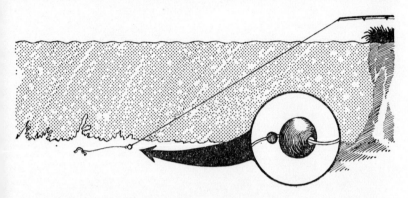

Fig. 29. LEDGERING   This is a simple method. A drilled bullet is stopped on the line by a split shot. The line is pulled through the bullet when the fish bites.

indicator and wait for a bite. By now you will know the habits of the fish so you will know how to deal with them. Figure 29 shows a simple method of ledgering.

It is usual, in such a book as I have written for you, to make a chart giving particulars of baits, sizes of hooks, line-breaking strain etc, applicable to every kind of fish, for easy reference. I am not going to do that. It is too easy. When you are experienced you will have no need of any easy references. Until that time, if you wish to know anything about the fish before you go fishing, you will have to read a whole chapter, then you won't forget the other essentials before you go down to the river. I am being a bit hard on you, am I? You will be glad of it one of these days.

Except for the pike fishing session and ledgering, we have talked only of float fishing, which is the basis of all good angling.

I want you to try your hand with the fly when you have had a little more practice with the float. Don't think that salmon and trout are the only fish which take the fly. Roach, rudd, dace, chub and the grayling will all take fly. And this brings us to part two of our book.

PLATE II   Comfortably seated in a good 'trotting' swim, this angler fishes
for dace on the Thames near Windsor

(*left*) This young angler, seen here checking the length of a small roach, is fishing to size limit

PLATE 12

(*below*) Holding the rod up keeps slack line off the water

Part Two

FLY FISHING

H

20

LET US GET A FEW THINGS STRAIGHT

You would like to do some fly fishing? Well, why not? You think that it will be too expensive and difficult, and you don't think you will be able to cope?

I wonder just how many people – old and young – I've heard say exactly the same thing. All I have to say in reply is simply one word – rubbish!

Let's talk about the expense of fly fishing. Naturally we think of trout and salmon when we talk of fly fishing, and that, in itself, is quite wrong. Trout and salmon are not the only fish which will take the fly. Grayling, chub, dace, roach, rudd and other coarse fish will take fly as readily as these.

I will admit that some trout fishing is very, very expensive, and to buy, or rent, a stretch of such water is far beyond the likes of me. I know stretches of some rivers which would cost thousands of pounds for a single mile. I suppose it is hearing about that sort of water which makes people jump to the conclusion that trout fishing is a millionaire's sport. Just you forget all about it.

You know, we often say 'this isn't fair' or 'that isn't fair' or 'why shouldn't I be able to have this or that when somebody else can have it'. But before we grow bitter let us take a look at this expensive water. To begin with it is easily accessible water, besides holding good fish. When people can afford to pay high prices for their sport they are usually getting on in years. They have acquired enough money to indulge themselves – and naturally they choose to fish in accessible water. Now you haven't lots of money, but you have legs, young legs, which will carry you to the not-so-accessible water, and that is water you can fish for next to nothing, or sometimes for no payment at all. Youth has vigour. So yours will be the wild streams, the tumbling waters of the remote countryside where the roar of motor traffic doesn't drown the mewing of the hawks in a clear sky, or the gay noises of fast water racing over stones.

The only rather expensive item of your fishing will be your rod and reel, for it isn't any use buying a cheap fly-rod. For that you must either save up or talk very nicely to your parents or grown-up relatives. I found when I was your age, that uncles were inclined to be the more sympathetic, but you know your own relatives better than I do, so you must plan your 'campaign' accordingly.

However, we will have a look at rods and tackle in due course.

Now we'll turn to the 'difficulty' of the gentle art of fly fishing. I think the idea that fly fishing is so difficult began years ago when many fly-fishermen were naturalists of considerable merit and entomologists of no mean order. The Latin name for this or that fly popped out of their mouths; they talked learnedly of the life cycle of the ephemeridae, the egg mass of the trichoptera, and so on which, of course, must have given the listener the impression that fly fishing was a very tricky business. Nowadays I do not think the average fly-fisherman has the same interest in entomology. Quite frankly I don't think it is at all necessary. The trout, or any other fly-taking fish, doesn't know, or care, whether the tit-bit it sees in the water is a nymph of any particular fly species, it just thinks it is something worth swallowing – and does so. Mark you, a certain amount of entomological knowledge will help you to understand more about the art of fly fishing, and it may well be an interest for the winter evenings, but to begin with it is not essential.

I have often been accused of over-simplifying the gentle art. I do not think I am at all guilty because it is very easy. I have a feeling that most fly-fishermen rather enjoy being regarded as something very superior.

Forget all you have heard about vertical casting, horizontal casting, false casting, etc., as being some kind of piscatorial magic. You will soon find out that there is nothing special in it at all.

Fly fishing is no more than offering an artificial fly to a fish, using a rod, reel and line to do so.

There are two types of fly fishing, wet and dry. A wet fly is one which is fished just under the water, and is therefore wet. The wet fly method is known to the dry fly purists as the 'chuck it and chance it' method, which I think is a bit snobbish, to say the least of it. The dry fly method is merely presenting a floating fly to the fish; hence the 'dry' fly. To keep the fly afloat it is oiled and the line greased.

If there is any real difficulty in either wet or dry fly fishing it is the method of correctly presenting the fly to the fish – in other words, the cast.

And yet I am unable to discover any difficulty that cannot be overcome by a little patience, a little practice and a sense of humour! When you begin to cast you will quickly see what I am getting at. All the same, if I could not teach the average teenage boy or girl to cast a reasonable line after six hours' tuition I'd be inclined to put my tackle up and fish no more.

All I ask of you is to read carefully all that I am going to tell you. I want you to learn it as you would your lessons for an examination. You will need to be patient with me because I shall take you, step by step, along the not-so-easy pathway which leads to efficiency. Naturally enough, you'll want to dash off and get on with the fishing, but if I were to let you, you would probably scare the wits out of every fish for miles around and end up disappointed and disillusioned.

Fishing, especially fly fishing, is a leisurely, patient sport. Take your time, and keep your eyes open.

I cannot promise to make you an expert fly-fisherman by asking you to read and learn what I am going to tell you. You can become expert only by your own efforts and further study and lots of practice. But I can promise you this: do as I ask you to do and you will then be able to cast a reasonable enough line to deceive some credulous trout, or whatever fish you may be after.

The number of fish you catch isn't important. Even if the rises are few and far between, there are other compensations. When I wander by a clear, fast-running stream, keeping my eyes open for a rising fish, or discovering a tumbling race of water spilling into a deep pool where the big one could be lying, I feel springy in the legs, and there's a good easy-to-breathe space in my chest and I am absolutely content. Nothing can touch me – worries, problems, petty irritations all dissolve into the clear fresh air. I am quite free and there is always the chance of a bit of sport to perfect the day.

21

FLIES

Now that we have established that fly fishing is not such a difficult art, one that is not beyond your abilities, and also that it is most certainly not a sport which only the wealthy can afford, there is nothing to prevent you from taking part.

Since we are to fish with the fly, it would be just as well, before we go any further, to know something about flies.

I am determined not to baffle you with science. Technique is the art of making a simple thing difficult. Let us keep to simplicity. We want no confusion.

When walking by a stream, have you noticed flies dancing over the water? Those flies are mating. After a little while the female will lay eggs, the eggs will sink to the bottom of the river and will, in the course of time, hatch and become flies too. When the flies have laid their eggs they will flop, exhausted, into the water and, if they do not drown, they will be gobbled up by some hungry fish. I want to make it quite clear that those flies which I have mentioned, and there are many varieties, are not the only flies that fish will gobble up. Bumble-bees, cow-dung flies, blue flies, grasshoppers – all sorts and sizes – are welcome to the hungry fish at the right and proper time, but it is the flies which come from eggs at the bottom of the river which are most important to the fly-fisherman.

The eggs remain in the mud of the river bottom until they hatch into insects encased in a kind of sheath. At this stage we call them nymphs. They struggle upwards, half-swimming, half-slithering, washed here and there by the flow and undercurrents of the river or stream until, eventually, they come to the surface. Up in the sun, they shed their sheaths. Their wings are freed and become dry.

Then they fly into the sunshine, mate and lay eggs, and the cycle begins all over again.

While the fly in the nymph stage is making its way upwards it does not go unnoticed. 'Nymphs for lunch today', says the fish and we need say no more! When it flops as a fly, upon the water, the fish says, 'Nice bit of fly going cheap', and that, too, is that!

There, I've kept that very nice and simple, haven't I? And I think it is enough for you to understand the difference between wet fly and dry fly fishing. In wet fly fishing, the fisherman uses an artificial fly which looks like the young in the nymph stage on its way up to the surface, and it must, therefore, be fished under water. Dry fly is an artificial fly representing the adult upon the surface.

Let us go a step further and examine these artificial flies.

Artificial flies are not made – they are dressed. Fly-fishermen never talk about making a fly. And when they talk of the 'pattern' they mean the way it is dressed.

What is used for dressing? Silk, fur, wire (silver or gold), feathers, mainly, and they are dressed as nearly as possible to look like the real thing. However, there are quite a number of 'fancies' which do not pretend to represent any particular fly, but are pure inventions. Yet fish take them. I suppose the best known of the fancy flies is the Wickham's Fancy. Trout, grayling, chub and dace will all take a Wickham's Fancy at the right time.

Just take a look at figure 30. First, the wet fly. Notice the eye of the fly is down-turned. Look, too, at the dressing. The hackle and/or wings are soft and pliable so that they become streamlined when fished to make it look as if the fly in its nymph stage is coming up to the surface. When the wet fly is 'worked' – we shall be talking of that later on – the down-turned eye makes all the difference to its underwater action, giving it the 'slithering' movement which helps to deceive the sharp-eyed fish.

Now for a dry fly. Apart from the eye being upturned, the essential difference is that the hackles are hard, otherwise it would not float. Those hackles come from a cock bird not less than two years old, so when buying dry flies, make sure the hackles are tough and resilient, otherwise it will be like fishing dry with a wet fly! Take notice, too, that the wings of a wet fly slope backwards, whereas the wings of a dry fly are cocked. Nowadays, alas – and I can't help feeling a little sad – the winged fly seems to have gone out of favour, being replaced by the hackled pattern. To my mind

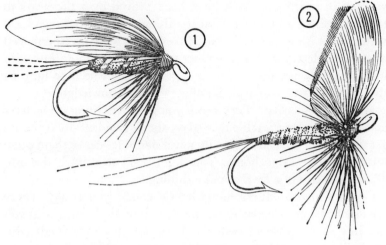

Fig. 30. FLIES   1. Wet fly.   2. Dry fly.

there is nothing prettier than the winged fly coming gently downstream. But the winged fly has an irritating way of getting itself waterlogged more easily than the hackled pattern, no matter how often it is dried and oiled. And it has a nasty knack of capsizing. So let me advise you, as a beginner, to plump for the hackled pattern every time.

There are many types of flies, and it is very difficult to know which to use and when. The appetite of the fish is affected by various conditions, weather and water is particular. On a coldish day, a fish won't take the same fly as it would on a warm day. When the water is low it won't fancy the same as when the water is fairly high. Then again, different streams may well have hatches of different flies. Of course there are flies which are good everywhere. There is the March Brown in the early part of the season. You can't go wrong there. And we have the Blue Upright, and the Pheasant-tail, both good from early on until the end of the season. We have, too, Wickham's Fancy for the warmer days, which is good in any stream or river. At the end of this chapter I will give you a list of the most popular flies, but I suggest you discover for yourself the patterns which have been proved over the years to tempt the fish – and under what conditions – upon your own local water. That is the way to learn. Make friends with an experienced angler. Anglers are always willing to help. Offer to go out with him, carry his net, his bag, to be a general dog's-body to him. In that way you will pick up a lot of very useful knowledge.

Are flies expensive? They are if you get them hung up in trees and bushes and are unable to retrieve them. Incidentally if you do get them hung up – and you will, never doubt it – leave them there until it is time to go home. You don't want to disturb the fish. The actual cost of a fly is about a shilling. . . .

Could you dress them yourself? Of course you could. There are any number of books upon the subject of fly dressing and you can buy an outfit from your tackle dealer at a very small cost. You will be able to copy all sorts of patterns and even invent your own special fancy, and that really would be something to write home about if it did the trick, wouldn't it?

I'll tell you about a friend of mine when we were at school together. He decided to dress his own patterns so he bought a book and the outfit. When he began he noticed that his sisters became interested, so he decided to put this interest to good use. He told them it was far too tricky for girls to do, which, of course, made them all the more eager to prove him wrong. They pleaded with him to let them try. At last, as if very much against his better judgement, he said he'd let them have a shot. And when they did he praised their work, said they were jolly good and he wouldn't have believed girls could be so clever. After that you just couldn't stop those girls dressing flies. And they were very good, as well I remember.

So, if you have any sisters, remember that girls are usually more nimble-fingered than boys. . . .

I hope that now there is nothing mysterious about the flies which, before very long, you will be using. As I told you in the beginning, it is all very simple.

Author's note

There has always been some controversy about what a wet fly is supposed to represent. My own opinion is that the fish takes it for a hatching nymph and I have written in that belief.

Wet Flies – Trout

Beginning of Season
March Brown; Greenwell's Glory; Blue Upright; Coch-y-Bonndu; Pale Olive; Blue Dun; Red Spinner; Red Spider.

Early Summer
Coachman; Olive Dun; Sand Fly; Black Gnat; Alder; Oak Fly; Red Quill Gnat; Wickham's Fancy.

Late Summer – Until end of Season
Red Ant; Red Palmer; Iron Blue; August Dun; Cinnamon Sedge.

Dry Flies – Trout

Beginning of Season
March Brown; Pale Olive; Blue Dun; Olive Quill; Greenwell's Glory; Alder; Blue Upright; Ginger Quill.

Early Summer
Wickham's Fancy; Orange Sedge; Alder; Pale Olive; Pale Evening Dun; Red Quill.

Late Summer – Until end of Season
Cinnamon Quill; Olive Dun; Red Quill; Wickham's Fancy; Silver Sedge; Orange Quill.

The Duffer's Fortnight (End of May – Beginning of June)
The Mayfly; Day Fly; Gad Fly.

22

ACQUIRING A BIT OF FISHING

IT ISN'T a scrap of good having rod, reel, line and the best of tackle if you have no water to fish.

Let us see how to go about acquiring that water.

First of all we can cheer ourselves up by realizing that there isn't a county in the British Isles where fishing is unobtainable. We have rivers, streams and lakes all over the place, and they all hold fish.

Naturally enough, as we are going fly fishing we have our eyes on trout water, though we must not forget that there are coarse fish which will take the fly and give us good sport.

As a beginning, if I were you, I'd have a chat with a fishing tackle dealer who will, almost certainly, know where to find good water at a reasonable price. And it isn't a bad idea to study an ordnance map and look up the small streams. Then get on your bicycle and do a bit of exploring on your own.

But let us examine other ways and means available.

First, there are the angling clubs. For a very little outlay, in some cases only a few shillings a year, you can become a member, and let me tell you right away that many of the angling clubs have bought up some very good water indeed.

Secondly, there is water to be had, usually private water, or belonging to some hotel or other, on the daily ticket principle.

Thirdly, free water which belongs to the town and is looked after by the town council. I know of two such stretches of water in Devon which, apart from holding trout and sea trout also hold salmon, and good salmon at that. Very likely there is a stretch of such water where you live. It is well worthwhile to find out.

Fourthly – and this is the best of all – private water. This water is usually the hardest to come by, and no wonder! The owner of a stretch of water is always pestered by people asking for a day's fishing. And if he granted every request he'd never have a chance of fishing himself. Nevertheless, the owner of such water does, very often, give a day's fishing – and it is to those who ask politely. Don't go barging in and demand a day as if it were your right. Believe it or not, I have come across people who seem to think they have only to demand and they'll get what they want. It doesn't work. If a person has bad manners he doesn't deserve to be granted favours, especially in fishing.

If you are lucky enough to live near the wild parts of the country, first-class fishing is yours for the asking. In the remote valleys, on the quiet moors, away from civilization, you will find the best water. Farmers will seldom refuse you. They only expect you to behave decently. This is the water I love best to fish. Wild turbulent streams full of racing stickles and deep pools where a half-pound trout fights with the strength of a two-pounder. And if you do not live near these streams, there are always the holidays. Do you know, I have never known a keen fly-fisherman who was unable to find a bit of fishing, which probably goes to prove the truth of the old saying: 'If you want a thing badly enough, you will get it.'

There is one more item of expense. It is very small, but should you happen to overlook it and be caught without it, then you would be in trouble. You must – no matter where you are – obtain a River Board licence to go trout fishing. It doesn't matter whether you fish private water or not. The licence is a must, so don't forget it. It will only cost you a few shillings every year and you can obtain it from most fishing tackle dealers or the post offices.

23

CHOICE AND CARE OF TACKLE

So FAR we have found that fly fishing isn't a rich man's sport; in fact we can acquire good fly fishing for very little payment indeed. But now we really are up against the money problem!

When buying tackle the most expensive way is that which appears at first to be cheap. Low-priced tackle will give little service and will let you down sooner or later. Good tackle – a rod and a reel will give you years of service. You will have to pay for it, but it is far cheaper in the long run.

Buy your tackle from a dealer of good reputation. A dealer who has a good reputation values his good name and only buys tackle made by a firm which also possesses a good reputation. That is very sound advice.

First we want a **rod**. A rod about 8 ft. will be just the one for you. Choose a split cane rod. If you had plenty of money I should suggest that you bought two rods, one for dry fly and one for wet fly. A rod built for dry fly is a little stiffer in its action than one for wet fly. But as you are economizing choose the dry fly rod. This will be quite adequate for the wet fly whereas a wet fly rod isn't so satisfactory for dry fly. You must realize, with dry fly, that you have always to cast upstream and if there is a wind blowing downstream, there has to be that extra bit of power to cast against it.

See that the tip ring and the butt ring are agate lined, and inspect the ferrules. I think you would be wise to choose suction joints: some of the lockfast and bayonet types always seem to be in the way and they only add weight to the rod. How does the rod feel in your hand? Does it lie sweetly on the palm? But you had better try that – indeed it is the only way – when the reel is fixed on.

How much will the rod cost? I am rather sorry to tell you that it will be all of ten pounds.

The **reel** is also rather expensive, for it will cost three to four pounds. Have it fixed to your rod to try for balance. Then when you have decided upon it, ask your dealer to show you how to take it apart, and what oil to use and when. There is one essential: make sure that your reel has a variable check. The check helps you to play a hooked fish. It is all quite simple. Your check puts a check on the fish. If your check equals the amount of strength a fish must use to take line from the reel in pounds, the constant strain will tire your fish. In the end it will become so exhausted that you will be able to bring it to your net. You may need to alter your check when playing a fish; therefore, the check on your reel must be easily adjusted – the mere touch of a finger should be sufficient. Again, your tackle dealer will be only too pleased to show you all you need to know.

Then there is **backing** which is cheap enough. What is backing? Let us call it running line. It goes on to the reel before the line proper which is dressed silk. The idea of backing is that if you have to give more line than your dressed silk line, the backing provides the extra length. But it is very seldom indeed that such an eventuality arises. The great advantage of backing is that it fills the reel, thereby enabling quicker reeling in, which is at times essential. 50 yd. of backing is only a matter of a few shillings. I advise you to ask your fishing tackle dealer to fix the backing to the reel, and then the dressed silk line to the backing. Watch how he does it.

Now for the **line.** Another quite expensive item. You will not have much change from three pounds. For dry fly fishing you should buy a double-tapered line. (The line begins to taper about 4 to 5 yd. from the ends and that means you can change the line around when it begins to wear.) These double-tapered lines are of different weights to suit the length and power of your rod. The tackle dealer will tell you the size your rod maker recommends. For wet fly fishing it is not necessary to use tapered line though it should be of dressed silk. And of course it is rather less expensive.

We need a **net.** A second-hand one will do, and I suggest that you select a folding variety. The net should not cost more than a pound, possibly much less.

Waders. You will, sooner or later, be obliged to use waders. You have three choices. First, knee-length, or just the ordinary wellington gumboot. They are serviceable enough in shallow water but being only knee high you will very likely have a boot full of water before you know where you are. Secondly – and I favour these – there are the thigh-length angler's rubber waders. But make sure they are studded. It is the easiest thing in the world to slip up when wading. The studs will help you to keep your feet. If money were no object then you would probably choose trouser waders with brogues. But as they are so very expensive we'll forget them.

Casts. You can buy a roll of nylon for half-a-crown and from it you can cut any amount of casts. And don't forget this: a cast should always be about three inches shorter than the rod. We shall see the reason for that later on.

Next we need a **fly case.** These are quite reasonable and I think you could pick up a second-hand one for a few shillings. But do not get one of those which are divided into little compartments with nice little perspex lids. They are all right indoors, but on the water when there is a breeze blowing you could lose quite a number of your flies. Buy a box in which you can clip the flies firmly.

Flies. About a shilling each – unless you dress your own.

Bag. I shouldn't spend much money on a bag – at least not in the beginning. You can carry all your tackle in your pockets, and thread your trout (if any) on a string for easy carrying. I like the old-fashioned basket creel myself. It is easily scrubbed clean after use which is a great advantage over bags which, despite detachable rubber linings, always seem to retain a fishy smell. You should be able to find a cheap, second-hand bag or basket creel fairly cheaply if you are set on one.

PLATE 13 A pair of surgical forceps is useful for gripping a hook firmly to remove it from a fish's jaw

(*above*) A young angler fishing for chub and barbel in the broken water of this small weir. There are many kinds of fish to be taken

PLATE 14 here

(*below*) An attractive corner of a Middlesex lake is an ideal location for the early-season tench

Gadgets. Never forget to keep a few pins stuck in the lapel of your coat. Quite often, the eyes of the flies will be 'gummed up' and a pin is the thing to clear them. Scissors and a knife are essentials. Tie a piece of red flannel on to them. That will save you a lot of time looking for them. Also ask for a butt spear.

Grease for line and oil for flies (**dry fly only**). This will cost only a shilling or two.

Finally, here is a little tip. It is a good idea to mark about ten inches on your landing net handle. You can then see if a trout you have landed is sizable. On practically all water, trout under a certain length must be returned.

Having spent so much money on tackle, we had better consider ways of looking after it, for, with care, tackle will last for ages. I use a rod which I bought twenty-three years ago and it is still in good shape. I have reels very much older than that.

To care for your rod is a very simple matter indeed. Whenever it has been used in the rain or damp air, you must wipe it dry before you put it away in the rod bag. The bag should be hung by its loop well out of harm's way. When the season comes to its end examine the rod carefully for cracked varnish. If you discover any cracks take it along to your tackle dealer to be re-varnished. When you are a little more experienced, re-varnishing is a job you can do for yourself, but at the moment you had better leave it to the dealer.

Next, your reel. You will remember how your tackle dealer showed you how to take your reel to pieces. You must take it to pieces every now and again and apply a spot of machine oil – the kind used for sewing-machines and typewriters. This will give your reel many extra years of service. Keep an eye open for little bits of mud or grit and remove them. There is nothing to beat grit for wearing out the moving parts of anything made of metal.

Lastly, your line. After a day's fishing dry your line. Never forget to do that, no matter how tired you are. You can go to the expense of buying a line drier, but the job can be done equally well by looping the wet part of the line over the backs of two chairs.

With the dressed silk line for dry fly fishing, note any small cracks or signs of wear, and rub them well with a small piece of uncooked mutton fat or a silicone preparation.

That is about all you have to do in order to ensure that your tackle will last. These simple measures will save you a great deal of expense and give you good sport.

24

ASSEMBLING THE TACKLE

BEFORE we go any further I think it is time that you tried your hand at tying the knots which every angler must know.

If all the fish that got away because of faulty knots were placed head to tail I wonder how far they would stretch? Never let it be said that you lost a good fish because you tied a knot badly.

Figure 31 shows three of the most useful knots. Take some pieces of string and practise tying them until you can do so with your eyes closed. And that isn't meant as a joke. You may well be fishing at night – especially when, later on, you will be after sea-trout – and if you can't knot without seeing you will be in trouble.

Keep practising in the odd minutes when you have nothing to do and you will soon become an expert.

It is very simple to assemble your tackle. Yet, all the same, people manage to find a wrong way of doing it.

Take the rod carefully from its bag. If it has been found that the ferrules of the joints are a little bit tight – which isn't a bad thing – grease them slightly with line grease and they will slip in quite easily. But don't forget to wipe them clean when you put your rod away. Now to assemble the rod. Place the butt on the ground and fix in the second joint. In doing this never, *never* grip the cane. Hold the metal part. And if you value your rod, do not twist or wrench. If your rod is a three-joint weapon, then in goes the third joint and there you are! The same care applies when taking your rod down. If your rod is equipped with suction joints give a gentle straight pull – no more.

Now fix your reel to the butt. See that it is firmly fixed. Nothing makes a fisherman look so stupid as when his reel parts company with the rod half-way through the actions of making a cast.

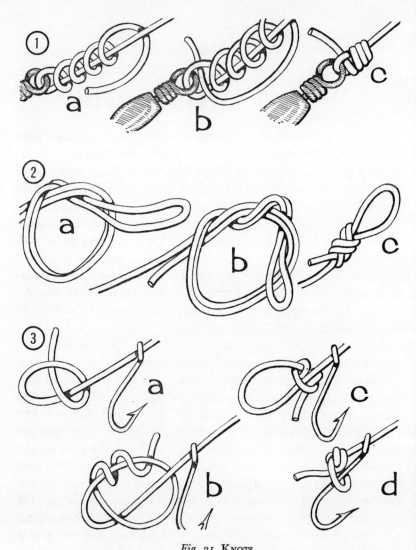

Fig. 31. Knots

1. *The four-turn half blood knot* (*a*) Line is passed through the swivel eye and turned four times about itself; (*b*) The free end is tucked through the turn nearest the eye; (*c*) The reel line is pulled to draw the knot tight on the eye. Trim free end.

Place your rod against a tree or any suitable rest, unless it is equipped with a butt spear which is a very handy gadget. You push it into the ground and it will save your rod from being trodden on. Next, thread the line through the rod rings. This is simple . . . providing the rings are properly aligned. Be quite sure that you don't miss a ring. It is the easiest thing in the world to do and it

Fig. 32. THE PROPER WAY TO CARRY A ROD

doesn't improve your temper, especially if you have tied on cast and fly.

Tie the cast to the line. Cut a length of nylon from the spool just about the same length as your rod. Now the loop. You know how to tie it and that makes your cast slightly shorter than your rod, which is as it should be. (If your cast is longer than your rod it might make landing a fish a little tricky. The nylon would have

2. *The double overhand loop knot* (*a*) An overhand knot is tied in a bight of line; (*b*) Add one extra turn to the knot; (*c*) Draw on both reel line and bight to tighten knot.
3. *The two-turn turle knot* (*a*) Thread fly on line and push clear of knot area. Turn as illustrated; (*b*) Turn the line twice around the bight; (*c*) Hold bight and draw on free end of line to tighten knot; (*d*) Tuck the fly and the free end of line through the bight, and draw on reel line to tighten knot about the fly.

to pass through the tip ring, which could cause a momentary check as you brought the fish over the net.) Now choose your fly and tie it to the cast. You know the right knot for this. There may be a small ring at the top of the butt into which the fly can be fixed. If not, press the hook well into the cork of the butt. It will be safe there. A hook stuck in a finger is not exactly an enjoyable experience.

The proper way to carry a rod is so that it *follows* you (fig. 32). This is the safest way for you are less likely to do damage to anyone coming towards you.

25

CASTING

WHEN learning to cast you really must have a sense of humour. You are going to find yourself in a dreadful mess before you have the way of it, and bad temper won't help matters. I can almost hear you say: 'And I was told it was easy!' It is, as you will find out. Just persevere and all will be well. Never mind if, at first, you find yourself tangled up with your line.

I will teach you the hard way which is the best in the long run. First, apart from your tackle, you need a book. Next you must find the place to begin – a lawn, a field, a yard – anywhere which is open.

Are you ready? Take your rod in your right hand and put the book under your arm; hold it tightly under your upper arm. You must not let it drop. Press your arm firmly to your body and keep it so.

There are two golden rules to remember. One is that you have a good rod so let the rod do the real work. Your job is to control the rod. Just that and no more. The second golden rule is never hurry the forward movement of your cast. Give the line time to extend itself fully behind you. Don't ever forget these two rules.

Let us begin. Look at figure 33. This is the proper way to hold your rod. You must control it with wrist and forearm; never the upper arm or shoulder. When a novice begins to cast he always wants to use the whole of his arm and shoulder. That would never do. Now you see why you have the book under your arm. If you go wrong – down falls the book.

How to stand? My own idea of the stance is only that it should be comfortable, easy and relaxed. What is easy for me might not be so for you. Just adopt a stance which suits you, possibly with your left foot slightly forward, and lean your body forward.

Having settled the stance we are ready for the next movement. I am going to try to teach you 'army fashion' – as a drill sergeant teaches a recruit rifle drill.

You are now standing at the ready position. Pull about 5 yd. of line from your reel which together with the cast make about 8 yd., and lay it out dead straight in front of you upon the

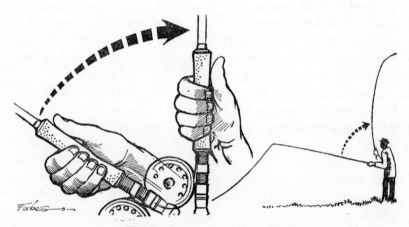

Fig. 33. CASTING   How to hold the rod.

ground and put a handkerchief just about 1 ft. in front of the fly. Now back to your original position and take another foot of line from the reel and hold it tightly, close to the reel, between the thumb and forefinger of your left hand. This must follow the movement of the reel.

The Backward Movement. Don't forget that the rod does the work. Bend your right knee slightly and with wrist and forearm only (keep that book tightly against your body), lift the rod fairly swiftly and smoothly, *ordering* it to carry the line backwards, then finish if off with a short sharp movement of the wrist. The passage of the rod must be slightly to the right of the shoulder – not straight back. This is very important indeed. Think of it in the way a sergeant would order recruits to slope arms. The long drawn out 'SLO-O-PE' would be as you were sending the line backwards, and the short sharp 'ARMS' would be when you finished the movement with your wrist.

Practise the backward movement until you have it right. You will get the feel of the rod, its power and energy, and you will sense the exact moment to bring the wrist into action.

The Second Movement. You have the backward movement right at last. You have sent the line smoothly behind you. And now you are ready for the second stage which isn't a movement at all. This is the pause which allows the line to travel backwards to its full extent.

Before you try this I want you to realize that the line must follow the movement of the tip of the rod.

You have taken the rod, in the backward movement, *outside* your right shoulder, therefore the fly must have described the right half of an elongated oval.

Now let us try the third and final – *The Forward Movement of the cast.*

The line has reached its full length behind you and your object is to send it forward so that the fly falls lightly at its original position about a foot short of the handkerchief. It is a good idea to aim your fly at a point *just above* the handkerchief, for that will ensure a gentle drop, or, when you are on the water, a gentle entry.

All set? Rise up slightly on the ball of the right foot, bring the right arm forward so that the rod passes close to the right ear (don't let that book fall!), almost back to the original position from which you made the backward movement – and then, just as line, cast and fly are about to come to the grass, the forearm drops down to the exact position from which you began the cast. See figure 34.

This is all there is to it, and by carrying out these instructions you should have made the perfect cast. Don't forget that pause between the first and final movements of the cast. Don't forget in the first movement to take the rod outwards and backwards, and in the third movement to bring the rod forward, close to the right ear. You will remember that, in taking the rod outwards in the backward movement, the fly, following the movement of the tip of the rod, must have described the right half of an elongated oval. Therefore, in the forward movement, when you bring the

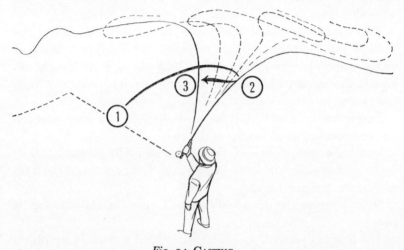

Fig. 34. CASTING

(1) Line on water. Lifted smartly to vertical, rod action takes line back to (2). Note the dotted lines showing how the line snakes back through the air, gradually straightening to reach (2). Rod punches forward to (3), follows through to (1) as line settles on water.

rod close to the ear, the fly describes the left half of the elongated oval.

You will now understand, as so many people do not, that a cast is not just a straight back and forward movement of the fly, for this would result in a nasty sharp crack and you would find that your fly had gone. You can also make nasty cracking noises by a jerky action even when the correct movements have been carried out.

The great thing to keep in mind when practising, is not to hurry your movements. Make them gently and smoothly, and before long you will find that the fly drops as gently as thistledown on exactly the right spot.

Once you can cast you will find it very difficult to purposely make a bad cast.

You have now mastered the vertical, or orthodox, method of casting. But it may happen that you are fishing on water where, because of overhanging trees, you cannot cast vertically. The alternative is to cast horizontally – the side cast. It is just the same as the vertical cast – the movements are exactly the same – but they are made horizontally.

Then there is the False Cast, which, as its name tells, is not a cast at all. All you have to do is to make the backward and forward movements of the vertical or horizontal cast two or three times without putting the fly on the water. The False Cast is merely used to dry your fly.

There are various 'fancy casts', the shepherd's crook cast, the cross country cast, and so on, but they are not for you yet awhile. Once you have mastered the vertical and horizontal casting you will be expert enough to fish in any water.

In your practising be content with casting a short distance; length will come as your skill increases. Never hurry. It won't be long before you have no need to lay line on the grass to begin your cast. You will be stripping it off the reel, sending it backwards and forwards with the confidence of a master fly-fisherman.

Casting is the most difficult – and infuriating – part of the angler's art to learn and accomplish, so let this be of some comfort to you when you find the going just a little bit rough. It would also be a help – even a comfort – to find some experienced fly-fisherman to assist you. He can give you his advice and point out where you are going wrong, as you practise casting. While I have done my very best to keep my instructions simple, words can never possess the clarity of the practical demonstration. I do not think you will ever come across an experienced fly-fisherman who will not be willing to give you the benefit of his knowledge and skill.

Oh, I almost forgot the Duffers' Fortnight! This is the fortnight when the mayflies appear in great numbers on a few chalk and limestone rivers and then trout go quite crazy and are easily caught – too easily for real sport. The Duffers' Fortnight occurs at the end of May and the beginning of June.

Forget the normal methods of casting when the mayfly comes (fig. 35). First there is 'dapping'. You place yourself under a tree where the trout are not likely to spot you. Push the rod out so that you can let the fly drop in the water, and then move it up and down slowly. You cannot fail to take good fish. Duffers' Fortnight seems a rather apt name, doesn't it? Then again you can try

Fig. 35. MAYFLIES

drifting. Keep well back from the water and let your mayfly drift downstream with the natural flies, never faster, never slower. Trout lose their cunning when the mayfly is about.

But there is one thing, when the trout goes for the fly count one . . . two before you strike. One . . . two . . . then strike, not before, or the odds are that you will be out of luck.

I shall tell you how to strike when the time comes.

Another method of presenting the mayfly is by blow line. You will need a rod about 14 ft. long – a bottom or coarse fishing rod – and a floss silk line on the reel. The rod is held at the perpendicular, and the line is floated over on the breeze, which is not what you or I would call casting.

By the way, if you can get hold of a book on entomology you might care to read about the mayfly. I never know whether to be sad for it or not. It spends two years as a grub on the river bed, and only one day in the sunshine on gauzy wings.

26

THE TROUT

QUITE naturally you are a little impatient to dash off to the water and try out your newly acquired skill in casting – without the book under your arm! But fishing, as we have said before, is no hurried sport, and it is a very good thing to know a little about the fish we are trying to catch. The more you know the better will be your

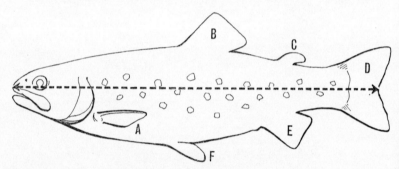

Fig. 36. TROUT – *showing the correct way to measure the length*
(A) Pectoral fins. (B) Dorsal. (C) Adipose. (D) Caudal or tail fin. (E) Anal fin. (F) Pelvic fins.

chances of success. Much of what I shall have to say about the trout will apply equally to those coarse fish which will take the fly: the grayling, chub, etc.

Trout spawn in the autumn. After eighty days the eggs become queer little creatures which we call trout alevin. Three weeks later the avelin is a little trout – called trout-fry – about ¾ in. long, and it has many many enemies. Herons, kingfishers, dippers and other fish, too, are only a few of the enemies of the tiny trout, and casualties are heavy, but this is the balance of nature, for if too many trout were left there would not be enough food in the rivers for them all. Trout also have an enemy amongst their own kind. He is the cannibal trout. He cannot be mistaken for he has a great head and a thin body, which proves that cannibalism provides little nourishment. His body will be a dark colour. There is only one way to deal with the cannibal – he must be killed for he is a menace! I have never known of a female cannibal trout, but that doesn't mean that there aren't any.

You will be able to tell the difference between the male and the female trout – or the cock and the hen, as they are called. The cock has a longer head with a prominent lower jaw, and his gill covers are pointed. The hen's head is smaller and neater, and her gill covers are round.

The trout grow rather slowly, taking two years to reach 8 in. Of course, the eventual weight and size of the trout is dependent upon the feed the river can provide. The chalk streams of Hampshire hold enormous trout because in those streams there is food galore. Whereas in the wild streams of the hills and moorlands a pound trout is a fish to talk about. But, oh my, a pound trout in a mountain stream knows how to fight! He'll give you some sport.

Not only does the river, or stream, govern the growth of its fish, it also governs their colouring. A fish's colouring is also its protection – designed by nature and it makes them difficult to spot in the water. Trout in murky streams are darker than those in clearer water and it is even possible to find trout of different colouring in the same river within a few yards of each other if the water varies in depth; the trout in a deep dark pool being darker than those in a shallower run a few yards farther downstream. Trout change colour automatically according to the colour of their habitation.

You know, of course, that all fish keep their heads to the flow of the water, facing upstream. The reason is that the fish takes water in its mouth, and as it flows through the gills so the oxygen is extracted, allowing the fish to breathe. Also food is brought downstream by the flow of water. Thus the fish is in the right position to take what comes to it.

But what is most important to the fly-fisherman is the trout's sight: particularly the Trout's Window or Cone of Vision. Now look at figure 37. It will be obvious to you that the deeper the trout lies in the water, the greater the area of its vision. Also it will be apparent that the nearer the surface the less it can see, even upon the river bank – note the angle of penetration. The window

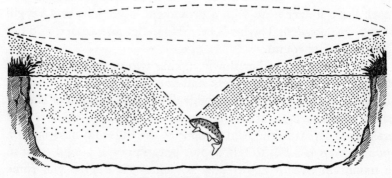

Fig. 37. CONE OF VISION

is, of course, circular since the apex of the cone falls upon the trout's eyes. Of course, all fish have their own cones of vision and while I cannot give the exact angles of penetration or the cover of vision for grayling and the other fly-taking coarse fish, the difference is too small to be of any importance.

There is one thing which you must not overlook, and it applies to dry fly fishing far more than wet fly. When you spot a fish rising to the fly note how near the surface it is lying. If you know that the fish has risen up from a depth beyond your sight, then you will know that he is likely to be able to see you standing on the bank. Cast from a kneeling position in the hope that you will be only a blur against the background.

You may hear that fish are colour blind, but I cannot find one

(*above*) Trout fishing with artificial fly. There is often a big one to be taken from the pool under a bridge

PLATE 15   (*below*) Netting a brown trout on the Itchen, in Hampshire. Note the pad on the angler's left knee for kneeling down while casting and watching for rising fish

PLATE 16   Wet fly fishing the small pools on the River Dart at Dartmoor

scrap of sound evidence to support such a belief. Some fish actually prefer flies of one colour and won't touch one of another hue. Just you try casting, say, a Wickham's Fancy when there happens to be a hatch of Blue Uprights. The fish know the difference between the ruddy hackle of the Wickham's Fancy and the pale blue hackle of the Blue Upright.

Can the trout hear? As far as you are concerned they do not, but they can feel vibrations which is why it is advisable to tread softly when approaching the water. It is also known that fish do possess the power to make noises which can convey alarm and warnings to others of their kind.

We know that trout have organs of taste and smell but it is very doubtful whether it affects their appetite for the fly. It is true that they vary in their preference for different flies, and our job is to present the fly they favour at the time.

It is a sad fact that trout are very prone to a nasty disease called Forunculosis. It is a deadly disease once it gets a hold in a river. Every fish affected is a carrier, so it will spread and do untold damage. If you catch a trout, or come across a dead one which has a darkish spot near the dorsal fin, or a red inflammation or spots between the anal and ventral fins you will know that the fish has the disease. There is only one thing to do – keep this fish and report it at once. If you are fishing on private water, take it to the owner, if in club water, to the club secretary. You must let it be known so there may be some chance of saving the fish still unaffected. This is your duty. And if you happen to have made a mistake – a false alarm – never mind. You will still have done the right and proper thing, which is always to your credit.

27

WHERE TO FIND FISH

No MATTER how well you can cast, no matter how realistically you present your fly, you will certainly stand a much better chance of success if you cast your line in a place where you know there is a fish!

How to spot fish will only come to you with experience and years of keen observation, and I believe, a sixth sense which you will develop as time goes on.

When you are fishing to the rise with the dry fly you will see the rise so you can't go wrong, but fishing with a wet fly, when you cannot see the fish (that is why wet fly fishing is sometimes called 'Chuck it and chance it'), then it is to your advantage to know the water favoured by fish.

And there is no golden rule to help you at all. Trout are quite unpredictable in their ways. Often you will find them feeding in the shallows with their dorsal fins almost breaking the surface, or sometimes they will be in the deeps, but generally speaking there are some parts of the water where they are much more likely to be lying than others. And it is for these parts that you must look.

Trout are not unlike humans in one respect. They want to get the most and the best of what they like with the minimum amount of effort. They choose a spot where the current will bring food to them. Then again, maybe being a little lazy and not caring to exert more energy than necessary in order to keep head-on against the stream, they will seek shelter. Behind a boulder is a likely place, or under some projection against the pressure of the current. We will cover those spots more fully when we discuss the way of wet fly fishing. For the moment I want you to acquire some little understanding of how to go about fishing wet before actually doing so. You will feel much more confident when the time comes.

Suppose we are walking beside the river, and we come across a stretch like this (fig. 38).

Do you see the boulders rising above the water? Notice how the current behaves after it has passed them. In this spot there will almost certainly be a fish.

Notice the flow of the current. The little back eddy is just the spot for a good fish to be feeding.

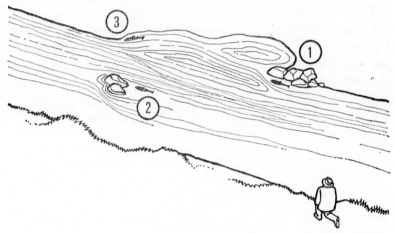

Fig. 38. A STRETCH OF WATER SHOWING THE PLACES WHERE THE FISH WILL BE FEEDING

Further upstream the water makes a U bend. How would you fish that water? Look at the current: note where it changes direction. Remember that we said trout will lie where food is brought to them, and also that they like protection from too strong a flow of water, especially when an eddy obligingly sweeps a tit-bit to them. It is a good thing to keep all that in mind whenever you happen to be walking beside water, so that you can exercise your mind by working out all the likely spots which will be chosen by trout. And the better the spot, the bigger the trout. Trout, like all the wild things on land or in water, only know one law, the law of might. To the strongest goes the best: in other words, the strongest trout is able to take the most comfortable position and the most food.

I am not saying you will find a fish every time in spots such as I have indicated: only that you are more likely to do so there than anywhere else. Trout, grayling, and other fish like a change just as we do. They aren't going to stay put in one place for the twenty-four hours of every day. We'll just say that they will spend most of the twenty-four hours in their favourite spot. A change of weather will give them the urge to change their position. I have taken trout, good fish at that, from the most unexpected and unlikely spots and I have no doubt I shall do so again. However, when we begin to fish with a wet fly we shall take all the possibilities into consideration so that in our casting we shall not leave much water unfished, in likely or unlikely spots.

28

THE FISH WE SEE

THE beginner is often tempted to try to catch the feeding fish which he can see. And that is not always advisable. So when you go fishing with the dry fly it will help if you are able to tell what a fish is doing by the movements of the rise.

To begin with it is much easier to spot the type of rise in smooth water, but with a little practice you will soon be able to do so in the more turbulent streams.

Some types of rise, unless you are aware of their significance, will lead you sadly astray and you can waste your time by the hour. You are fishing with a dry fly, therefore it is essential you should know by the rise if the fish will take your fly when presented.

Let us take a look at the rises which will deceive the novice angler.

First, and the most common, is the 'bulger'. This fish shows its shoulders and breaks the water with its dorsal fin. That should tell you that the bulger is feeding on the immature flies before they reach the surface and become properly winged. It is not impossible to take such a fish with a dry fly, on the principle that nothing is impossible. However, if you will take my advice you will leave it alone. Your chances of sport, as far as the bulger is concerned, are practically nil.

Then we have the 'tailer' and this is no better. It grouts about among the weeds, feeding on fresh-water shrimps, snails and the like. Its tail is up, breaking the water, and its head is down. Let it get on with its tailing, no matter how tempted you may be.

Other time-wasters are the 'smutting' trout. We say they are smutting when they are feeding on the clouds of midges which often descend upon the water – and us!

It is, perhaps, not so much a waste of time to try for the smutters as for tailers or bulgers, but I usually leave them alone. The one trouble is that you will have to fish so fine and with such a small fly – a black gnat is my fancy – that the chance of getting a good fish to your net isn't particularly good.

It is not a good thing to hook trout, or other fish for that matter, and then lose them. Fish aren't fools, you know, and it doesn't take long for them to regard flies with a great deal of suspicion. You don't want to make fish fly-shy!

And now we come to the arch tempter, the 'cruiser'. Even after all the years I have fished I still have quite a job to refrain from trying my luck.

Fig. 39. THE BUBBLE RISE

The cruiser is the trout – and frequently a very fine fish too – which swims round and round and round a pool, rising here, there or anywhere to whatever fly is on the water. And as this fish is visible it is an awful temptation to try to take it. I won't say you cannot take a cruiser. I have done so, but it is a very, very chancy business, and most certainly not worth the time.

The rises that promise sport are those which the novice must recognize. The 'sucking' rise must never be missed. Fish it! You see the rings in the water radiating outwards, and in the centre a bubble, the bubble telling you where the fly has been (fig. 39).

Then there is the 'sip' or 'small sucking' rise which is made generally under the bank, or beneath a tree. This rise is well named because it is made so very quietly that the water is barely disturbed. The fish simply pushes its upper lip above the water and sucks in the fly floating downstream. Keep your eyes open for the sip and if you hook the sipping fish, be ready for fireworks. You may be fast into a fish which is really worthwhile. After all the years I have fished, even now, when I hear and see a 'sip' rise, the thrill comes back. Is it that monster I've been waiting all my life to catch? Never, never miss a 'sip' rise!

Watch for the 'head and tail' rise. You will see the fish breaking the surface with its head as it takes the fly and then again as it dives down, with its tail.

Fig. 40. THE ROLL

The most graceful rise, and one I dearly love to see, is the 'roll' (fig. 40). Unfortunately the trout doesn't often indulge in that form of rise, which is a pity, for not only does it please the eye but it also denotes a fish which will take your fly.

One more form of rise that you will come across is the 'slash'

Fig. 41. THE SLASHING RISE

(fig. 41). This is when the trout, fearing it is going to lose some fly or insect, makes a rush and is carried by its own speed, partly out of the water. But without your knowing for certain what the trout is after – alder fly, sedge fly, or mayfly – there isn't much point in trying for the 'slasher'.

That, I think, covers the rises which you must learn to spot, but do remember that **any** form of rise which makes rings and contains a bubble, or bubbles, tells of a rising fish that will take the fly.

You will find it very simple to tell one from the other, but do be careful not to be swayed by the temptations of the time-wasters.

Yet I have a feeling that they will, now and again, lead you astray as they have done so often with me.

29

ESSENTIAL THINGS TO KNOW

BEFORE we go to the water we had better run over one or two essentials so that we know what we are doing, and how to do it. We will begin with **Greasing the Line.** If you are to fish with a dry fly then the line must float and the way to keep it afloat is by simply applying grease. At one time, when I was your age, uncooked mutton fat was the stuff we used and of course red deer fat. I still hear old timers like myself proclaiming the advantages of red deer fat, but, even if you *can* get hold of some, I think you had better leave it alone. It contains salt and salt will not do your line any good. There are many first class preparations on the market and your tackle dealer will give you good advice. Grease your line often and well. Smear the grease around it and then rub it well in with a small piece of soft leather; or smear a little grease on the leather and rub it into the line. I do not need to warn you against greasing your line when it is wet!

Oiling the Fly. As the dry-fly fisherman makes the line waterproof to keep it afloat so he must do the same to the fly. Here again, your tackle dealer will be able to supply you with the right preparation.

Oiling the flies the night before you go fishing is a bit of sound advice, but never under any circumstance try to oil a fly which has become water-logged or even wet!

False casting will help you to keep your fly dry. But once it gets really wet, for the oil will not keep it water-proof indefinitely, there is only one thing to do – use a fresh fly. A fly can be dried to some extent by gently squeezing it in your dry handkerchief. A silicone preparation is sold which is excellent for dry flies.

Returning a Fish to the Water. This is something you must know how to do. When I see a fisherman returning a fish to the water I can tell you just what sort of fisherman he is from the way he goes about it.

Fish are returned because they are either undersized or the fisherman wants to catch them again another day. But it isn't much use returning a fish to the water if, when doing so, you do it so much harm that it dies. I have seen fish actually thrown back into the water. Fish are cold blooded and being gripped in a warm human hand comes as a bad shock. Put your hand in the water before gripping the fish, or, if you have a cloth to hold the fish, soak it first.

Fig. 42. WADING

Take the fish firmly in your hand and remove the fly with a quick twist. Then hold the fish underwater, head upstream, for a minute and then open your hand. If you return a fish in this way it will live to give you sport another day.

And now – **Wading.** Now that we have all sorts of waders we are able to keep our feet and legs dry.

When wading, keep in mind the fact that fish lie with their heads upstream, therefore if you are wading downstream you will be spotted by the fish (fig. 42). This means casting a longer line unless you wade close to the bank and fish across and downstream and cover the water that way.

On the other hand, when wading quietly upstream, it really is quite remarkable how near to a rise you can get – providing one is facing the sun and the shadow is cast behind.

Often I fish a stream in Herefordshire called the Olchon – a hill stream which has to be waded. There is one stretch where the water suddenly deepens and I can wade no farther, so there I stop and fish, keeping quite still. And every time I reach that spot I disturb a certain fish which weighs almost ½ lb. In under ten minutes back it comes and takes up its normal position less than a yard from my legs. I shall never try to catch this fish. I hope no one else does.

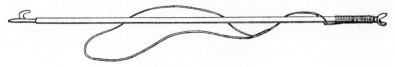

Fig. 43. WADING STAFF

However, when wading – and this applies especially to water which you do not know – watch your step! It is not at all difficult to slip and it is not at all difficult to walk thoughtlessly into four or five feet of water.

A good wading staff is very useful (fig. 43). You can pay a fancy price for one but I make my own and so can you – with very little trouble. A stout, straight length of ash is just right for this purpose, so keep your eyes open for one when you are out and about in the country. Wrap some lead sheeting around the bottom to help to keep the stick down when you let it swing loose when casting. You can fix the little hook arrangement on the top without much bother, for it will come in useful when you have a fly hung up in a bush or a tree. For the sling, I suggest you get some picture-hanging cord and give it a coat of varnish, and, of course, give your ash stick a good coating of varnish too. Use your wading stick to feel your way along so that you can judge the depth of water as you wade.

By the way, after a day's fishing, look after your waders. If they are rubber boots, turn the tops back and lay them on their sides so that they will dry out for moisture will have formed inside them during use. Then hang them up.

If you have the stocking waders, turn them inside out to dry and, as with the rubber boots, hang them up too.

We are now ready to go down to the stream to put our first fly on the water.

30

WET FLY FISHING

BEFORE we set off for the water let us make absolutely sure we have not forgotten any item of tackle.

Once we reach the waterside we must do some more remembering. You know all about it. Walk gently, don't allow your shadow to fall on the water and do not stand against the sky line. These are essential if you are to have any sport.

Put your rod together, tie the cast to the line and select your fly.

And before we begin let me give you a little more advice, and very sound advice too. In all sports and games the sportsman or player who excels must be able to concentrate on whatever he is doing to the exclusion of all else. The batsman who, for one fleeting second, takes his eye from the ball, finds his wicket spread-eagled; the goalkeeper who looks the other way finds the ball in the net; the boxer who is distracted for a split second and drops his guard ... well, you know what happens to him!

If you are to catch trout, not for a second must you allow your attention to be distracted from your angling. It always seems to happen that when you take your eyes from the fly for one jiffy, just at that moment the best trout in the water takes the fly ... and you miss it!

On the water there are more distractions than anywhere else I know. A bright kingfisher comes skimming downstream. Or a dipper perches on a stone and does his bobbing and bowing act. Perhaps there is a plump little vole sitting in the duck-weed, nibbling the choicest bits between its little pink paws. There are so many beautiful things to enjoy that it is difficult to concentrate, and I will admit I cannot always do so myself, but at least we can try.

We will fish downstream with the 'chuck-it-and-chance it', or the wet fly way of fishing. This has one very great advantage where the beginner is concerned. Should he make a poorish cast such as would put a fish down if he were fishing with a dry fly, it doesn't matter. The current will mend his cast and carry it to where it should have gone. On the other hand fishing downstream has some disadvantages too. A fish lies with its head upstream, therefore, it follows that when it takes the fly and the fisherman strikes, he is 'twitching' away from the fish's mouth. This accounts for the number of fish which, although they are taking the fly, are not hooked. The other disadvantage is that when fishing downstream, the fisherman comes within the fish's vision sooner than he would when fishing upstream. This means he must cast a longer line.

Now then, how to go about fishing a wet fly downstream. Make the cast across the stream at just short of a right angle. The current does the rest. Have a couple of loops of line on your left hand, between thumb and forefinger, so that you can let it go and lengthen the cast. The current is really most obliging to the wet fly fisherman. Your fly has reached the lie, or point that you have chosen. Now begin to fish.

Remember what we said earlier about the wet fly? We thought that the wet fly represented a hatching nymph, struggling upwards with a slithery swimming movement, on its way to the surface to shed its sheath or case. So you must 'work' your fly to give it that slithery swimming movement as you bring it in with reel or by hand. You must 'sink and draw'. To sink the fly, lower the point of your rod for a few seconds, and down it goes. Raise your rod for a few seconds, and up it comes. All the time you are drawing it in towards you. While you are doing that, providing the water is calm, try to make the tip of your rod do a little tremble to add extra realism to your fly's progress through the water.

Now you have the idea, but there is far more to it than just a simple cast: you must plan to cover the water, taking very special note of the spots which are lies.

You must go about it in such a manner that you will not disturb your fish unduly. It stands to reason that if you hook a fish which is farthest away from you, landing that fish will disturb those which are closer to you and they will be lost to you for the time being. When you select the water which you intend to fish, you must bear in mind those features which we have already discussed and which give promise of holding good fish.

Look well at figure 44.

Begin your casting at A and finish at B. In this way the water will be covered.

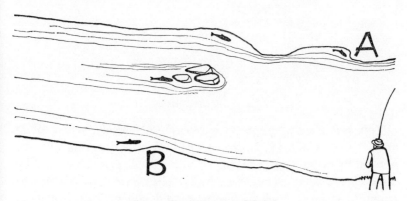

Fig. 44. COVERING THE WATER

You are fishing with one fly only, but many anglers, when fishing with wet fly downstream, use more than one fly. In a small stream two is the usual number, but on sizable water, three or four are frequently used.

Tail fly and droppers are used by experienced anglers. The droppers are kept short otherwise they are apt to tangle. A clove-hitch is used for fitting a dropper to the cast (fig. 45).

And now, having told you about droppers, I suggest that you forget all about them for a while. As a beginner you will have quite enough to keep an eye on one fly. The idea of using more than one fly in a cast is in the hope that if one fly doesn't appeal, one of the others will. This is logical enough, but what is wrong with changing your single fly until you hit upon the one that matters? That, again, is just another of my own practices, but let us get on with our fishing.

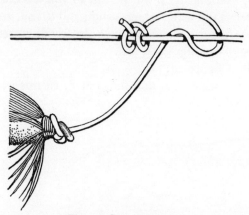

Fig. 45. CLOVE-HITCH

You are bringing your fly in, working it nicely, when all at once it begins to drag. No trout will look at a dragging fly. The natural fly doesn't drag! Dragging is inevitable and it is caused by the pull of the current carrying the fly. The currents are of different strength or flow. Look at figure 46 and you will see just what

Fig. 46. FLY DRAGGING

happens. Sometimes this can be overcome by using the wrist to take the belly out of the line and straighten it up, but this doesn't always work and I am inclined to try casting from another position.

You are fishing blind, which means that you cannot see a fish. You are also drawing the fly away from the fish. When a fish takes a fly it opens its mouth and if the taste or feel isn't right the fish blows it out again. That is why, when fishing wet, we often feel a sharp tug . . . and then nothing. The fly has been taken and rejected and we are too late to do anything. However, if you keep your eyes really skinned, and you know where to look, you may get just a quick glimpse of silver gold as the trout takes.

As soon as you feel the tug or see the fish take the fly you must strike. Striking is simply a flex of the wrist, keeping the line taut with thumb and forefinger of the left hand. It isn't easy. You may strike too late, too soon, too hard so that the hook is torn from the fish's mouth or you may break your cast. But soon you will develop that sixth sense which tells you when and how to strike. And often the trout helps you. When fishing wet you are pulling the fly away from the fish, who chases it, thinking it will get away from him. He makes a dash, takes the fly, turns . . . and the impetus of his rush does the rest. He is hooked!

I am sure that the taking of most trout on wet fly is due solely to the trout's determination not to allow a tit-bit to escape him.

This should encourage a beginner quite a lot!

To fish upstream with a sunken fly you need to grease your line for we must keep it floating; it is your fly that you wish to sink – although not more than an inch beneath the surface – so you must not oil it as you would a dry fly.

When fishing upstream you have two advantages over fishing down: you can get close to the fish, which means a shorter cast; and when you strike you will not be twitching the fly away from the fish's mouth. But don't make a hash of your cast! When fishing downstream the current will put a bad cast to rights, but upstream the current offers no help at all. Just because you are able to approach your fish from behind, don't think you may not give your presence away. It is the easiest thing in the world to let yourself be spotted. Think what you are doing and never forget to tread lightly. And it is now that you may have to exercise all that patience which is supposed to be the angler's own special virtue. It is absolutely essential to present the right fly when fishing wet upstream – and I am sticking to that whatever anyone may say. If you have the right fly with the first cast you will be lucky. If you have not, try another – and another – until the trout lets you know that you are offering the right pattern. Then the sport will be yours.

When upstream fishing you will have the advantage of seeing the trout take the fly. You will – if you keep your eyes wide open and your concentration does not waver – see the quick under-water turn, the movement of a 'shadow' fish or the gleam of the golden flank. Then the trout has taken your fly. Remember the trout sucks in and blows out. Strike on sight; a quick flex of the wrist. There are more fish lost, when fishing wet upstream, by striking too late than too soon.

It has just occurred to me that I haven't said much about fishing upstream with the wet fly, but there isn't a lot to say on the subject. It is the method of fly fishing which demands knowledge and experience – and experience I cannot give you. I have tried to tell you where and why fish choose their lies. You know how to cast. The rest is up to you. Always keep your eyes open and ponder over all you see by the waterside. Ask the questions, find the answers . . . and you will become a fly fisherman worth knowing!

31

DRY FLY FISHING

DRY FLY! There is a little bit of magic in the very words. And now you have come to the time when you will be casting a dry fly yourself! Don't forget that greased line and the oiled flies.

Dry fly fishing is governed by the nature of the water you are to fish. Let us take the southern streams and rivers. There you will have the 'hatches of fly'.

These hatches – with an accompanying wholesale feeding time for the fish – occur mainly between eleven in the morning and two in the afternoon, and, in summer, just before dusk. They may last any time from a few minutes to as much as an hour. Feeding time begins quite suddenly – a rise here and there and then they really tuck in. And they stop quite suddenly. It is almost as if a gong has been sounded or a cry of 'Dinner up! Come and get it!' and then another cry of 'That's all for now: more later'. After that there is quiet, though the occasional feeding fish is still to be seen. You haven't forgotten the chat we had about the significance of 'rings' and 'bubbles'?

In the small wild and turbulent moorland streams where there is seldom, if ever, a hatch of flies to be seen, the trout rise almost all the time but you have to spot them before you can fish them, and that is when your knowledge and gift of observation comes in.

Before we go any farther, let us have one or two good rules to observe and keep. When you spot a rising fish – keep directly behind him.

Cast your fly so that it falls a couple of feet above your fish and so that it comes nicely downstream over the centre of his window.

If you are pestered by drag – as well you may be, since it is so very often unavoidable – you can do one of two things: (*a*) mend the line; (*b*) leave the fish. I prefer to do the latter. There will be fish rising elsewhere and ten to one, by trying to mend the line you will only succeed in scaring your fish away.

Now, let us fish a rise. Don't take any chances. Make a Red Indian approach to the water. Keep down! Do your casting from the kneeling position. You have already chosen your fly – which you have oiled, or should have done – the night before. You select the rising fish. You must not make a mess of it. Try two or three false casts for distance. There is no need to hurry. The trout is feeding, rising steadily, quite unhurriedly, to one fly after another. Take your time.

You make a good cast. The fly drops gently eighteen inches to two feet above his head! It is coming downstream . . . just right . . . no drag. You are going to rise that fish – you can feel it in your bones!

But just a moment – let's do some quick thinking. We can't afford to make a hash of the strike. We have been fishing with a wet fly. We have had to strike as quick as a flash. The situation now is not quite the same. I will tell you just what that trout you are angling for will do. I'd say that he is roughly ten inches to a foot below the surface and he is in no hurry. Also he has been looking into his window for flies for some time. He will have seen yours, never fear. That trout will bide quietly watching your fly come along to him and not until it is a matter of inches from his nose will he move. He is a feeding fish; slowly he will rise up to the surface and at a slight angle, open his mouth and gently suck the fly in. And just as gently he will close his mouth, turn and sink down again. Naturally he will spit out the fly when he discovers that it is not a true fly, but he will not do so as quickly as a fish in turbulent water – especially with a wet fly. Therefore you take a little longer over the strike. You see your fish's 'nose' break the water. Give him a short second to turn and, as he does so, make a mere twitch of a strike and you are fast into him. Keep that in mind whatever else you may forget. I have seen good trout lost by striking too soon when fishing dry, just as I have seen some good ones lost through striking too late when fishing wet.

Now all that I have told you so far applies to the rising fish on fairly smooth water – during a hatch or at any other time. You see the fish and you know the way to take him. But we may not be fishing calmish water where we have a twice daily hatch of fly. We may be fishing the tumbling mountain and moorland streams where there is no hatch and a rising fish is hard to spot in the broken water.

Here in these streams, because we cannot always see the rising fish we must remember all we have learned. Once again, as in fishing the wet fly upstream, it is a matter of knowing the kind of spots the fish will choose for their lies. But remembering that the trout likes a change, don't give up if you have no luck in a suitable lie. Cover the water; leave nothing to chance.

You already know of their likely lies. Keep your eyes on them. Even if there is no visible rise in fast water, remember that there are no twice daily hatches and the fish may feed at any time. Present a fly and find out. If one fly doesn't tempt them, another one may.

You are bound to be bothered by drag, more so than in gentler water. The drag in fast water is not so fatal to your fishing as in the gentler water. The drag may mend itself and your fly may smoothly cover a fish a little farther downstream . . . nearer your feet!

Let us take a run coming from a deepish pool. Another word for a run is a stickle. Most likely the best fish are in the deeper water, but the fast shallow water should not be overlooked. Fish up to the pool. Trout will drop back from the deeper water to take the fly on the tail, or end, of the stickle.

You will, almost without doubt, miss many rises, which will not be your fault. When the water is fast the fish's window is not as clear as it is in gentle water and the trout quite frequently misses the fly altogether. He is eager to take the fly. It is coming towards him very quickly but his vision isn't too clear so he misjudges the distance as he comes up to take. Unless you feel a slight tug which tells you have pricked him – cast again. The odds are that he will have another go.

However, you may miss the fish because you have struck too late. If you keep your eyes on your fly, you will have a quick glimpse of the dark shadow, golden flank or white belly, as the trout takes. You must strike immediately. You have precious little time.

When fishing the fast water, never pass an eddy, especially one under the bank, without putting a fly on to it, even if there isn't a sign of fish movement – especially an eddy which has become scum-covered. The trout knows a trick or two. When the nymphs of the flies are struggling upwards they get themselves stuck on that scum and they can't rise up from the water. They have to remain where the trout can take them at his leisure. I am not suggesting that you should try to fish an eddy covered with thick scum which looks like soap suds, but the thin almost transparent scum will often be the place to take a really big trout.

And the same goes for a nice smooth run beneath overhanging branches. The big one could be there, ready to take the fly.

A run between two banks of weeds should not be overlooked either, despite the probability of a drag.

32

PLAYING A TROUT

It makes no difference whether the trout has been hooked on a dry fly or a wet fly when it comes to playing it. You are faced with the fact that neither your rod nor your cast is made for yanking a hooked fish clean out of the water. Your job is to play that fish; or in other words, to tire it out so that you are able to lift it from the water in your landing net.

The golden rule when playing a trout is simply to keep your line tight. And before we go any farther there is one more little fact which is not at all to your advantage. While a trout will very seldom make a dash of more than twenty or thirty yards from its lie – and that means you will always have ample line left on your reel – you know nothing about underwater conditions. But the trout knows just where all the snags are to be found: the submerged tree roots, and other spots around which it can twist the line. And, of course, there are weeds. If it is possible to inspect the water when it is very low, as it so often is during July and August, you will probably catch sight of the odd snag, and when the day comes to play a fish you will have a bit of very useful knowledge. A fisherman must keep his eyes open at all times, and he must have a good memory.

We shall now go back to the playing of the trout. The fish is firmly hooked. Your job is to turn the fish's head downstream as soon as possible, and for two good reasons. A fish, as you will recall, lies with its head upstream so that the water passes through its mouth and out of the gills, thus enabling it to breathe freely. When you turn its head downstream breathing becomes rather more difficult. This, quite naturally, tires a fish pretty quickly. Again, there will probably be more trout in the water a little higher up. You don't want your hooked trout dashing about amongst them and giving them a scare. Keep a steady strain on your fish. If you have to give your fish line, keep your rod point well up. The weight of the line itself will do its work. Here is the general principle: a fish is pulling your line off the reel at a strength equalling, say, 1 lb. The breaking-strain of your cast point is $1\frac{1}{2}$ lb., so the cast will not be broken. The check on your reel must never impose a brake of more than the breaking-strain of your cast point. Do get that firmly into your head – otherwise you will hear some nasty pinging noises which spell, very loudly, broken cast and lost fish!

To continue with the action – your fish has made a dash, tearing yards of line off the reel and all at once the dash comes to an end. Gather in your line, keeping it tight. Never give the fish the slightest respite from the strain. There will be another dash; be ready for it. The trout will dive into the deeps, boring down as only a trout can. But gradually the trout begins to weaken. It will not give in whilst it has a scrap of strength left. Now is the time to put the real pressure on. Push the butt of your rod towards the fish. It will bring the point over your shoulder slightly and will put the greatest strain upon the fish. Barring accidents, or a little carelessness on your part, the fish should be yours, and for the moment we can leave it. The playing of that fish was just a straight-forward job, free of complications. But there are times, as you will come to know, when it will not be a straight-forward job, by a long way. Let us take the trout that, when hooked, 'flaps' on the surface. That one will, in all probability, be lightly hooked, so in holding fast there is a very real chance of tearing the hook from its mouth. On the other hand if you hold on gently there is just a very slight chance the hook may embed itself deeper. It can only be a matter of choice. Either way, you stand a really good chance of failing to bring the fish to the net; in fact I'll go farther and say you will lose five out of six such lightly hooked fish whatever you do. But what does it matter? If the fish gets away it will live to fight another day, and that in itself is a very good thing.

Now suppose you hook a good-sized fish in a pool and that you have certain knowledge which you share with the trout. You both know there are some submerged tree roots under the opposite bank. The trout is hooked and away it goes, straight for those roots. What are you going to do about that? You must take a risk. If you let that fish get into the roots you have lost him for certain. Try to turn him. It is a risk, for your line may part. You must put on side-strain. Lower your rod from the vertical to the horizontal and turn the point away from the fish. It is the only way, and I would say you have just slightly more than an even chance of turning the fish. Now you have him away from the roots; up goes the point of your rod and you carry on playing in the normal way.

Another way the trout fights for freedom is by jumping high and clear of the water. If that fish flops back upon the line it is quite likely that the fly will be torn from its mouth. Also if you happen to be holding the line very tightly the result will be the same. Whenever a trout jumps *towards* you, *lower* the point of your rod and when it jumps *away* from you, *raise* the point of your rod.

Never be afraid to fight the hooked trout. I have seen so many good fish lost purely because the fisherman has been too nervous, for one reason or another, to put the pressure on when he should. Let a fish get the better of you, and you have lost it for certain. I don't mean that you should use brute force. I am all for the gentle but firm playing of a trout, but when the time comes and a risk must be taken – take it.

Trout feed, as you know, very often between weed banks. If you hook one of those fish you will soon see what will happen if you are at all timid. You have only one chance. Put the maximum strain on as soon as you have made the strike. Turn that fish, get his head downstream, the further away from those weeds the better. It is the only way. When strain is put on a fish in this situation he will often jump the nearest weed bank and come into clear water!

I think we have covered the problems of playing a trout. If you will commit what I have written to memory and act upon it, you

157

will not go far wrong. A trout is never ours until we have him on land, and a good few yards from the water, at that – with which thought we must come to the final phase of our battle with a trout: the use of the landing net. A very simple job and yet ... but we'll deal with that in the next chapter.

33

LANDING THE FISH

NETTING a played-out trout should be the easiest job in the world. There is the fish absolutely dead beat with apparently not a kick left in him . . . and yet . . . oh dear! It is easy – if only the angler would do the job the *easy* way.

You must never try to land a fish with a dry net. A dry net is apt to float and that won't help at all. Give the net a good soaking before you have need to use it. When I was a boy, although I was well aware that I should soak my net, I very often did not. I was a little bit superstitious, believing that it was tempting providence – that I was being too sure I should hook a good fish. And as a result I lost more than one good fish. Don't be superstitious – being prepared is much more profitable. A floating net does not sink under the fish! Another important thing to remember is to keep calm. The sight of a really good fish often upsets the confidence of quite experienced anglers. Never jab the net at the fish. That is the way to knock it off the hook.

The only safe way to land the fish is to sink the net deeply and bring the fish quietly up to and over it. But you must *not* attempt to lift the net until the fish is well and truly over the centre. And, as you lift with a nice clean steady hoist, let your line go slack, for the fish will have a good last kick when in the net, which can damage your cast (fig. 47).

Now that you have your trout well and truly in the net you must decide what to do with him. If it is a matter of putting him back you know how that should be done. But suppose you want to keep him, for after all a trout makes a very tasty dish! You don't want him to die slowly so you must kill him, and it is kinder to do it quickly. If you have a priest (the correct gadget for killing a

159

fish) all well and good, but a fair-sized stone, round or flat, will do it just as well. A sharp rap at the back of the head – and it is all over!

Before you can cook the trout you must clean it. Lay the fish on its back, and push a sharp knife through the gills, cutting the gill covers clear at the throat. Then make a cut lengthwise down the belly, between the pairs of fins, as far as the vent. Cut away from

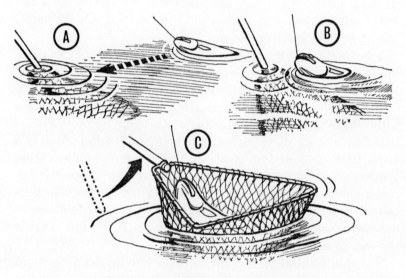

Fig. 47. THE CORRECT WAY TO USE A NET

yourself for safety. Put a finger inside the gill covers and remove the gills themselves. Remove the entrails from the belly. Now wash the fish thoroughly and let it dry. Remember that a trout should always be served with its head intact.

I like my trout grilled. Rub the inside of the fish with a little salt, dip it in flour to which salt and pepper has been added. Place the fish on the grill, dab it with butter and proceed to grill. Another way is to cover the trout with egg and breadcrumbs and fry it in butter. Next, beat two ounces of butter into a cream, add a tablespoonful of chopped fennel, a pinch of salt and a little black pepper, and a teaspoonful of lemon juice. Beat well and make into pats. Serve a pat with each fish.

Steamed fish, especially if they are over a pound in weight, are good, especially if they are served cold with salad.

If you want to send a brace (that means two) of trout through the post, rub salt into them and wrap them in grease-proof paper. Do not put them in a polythene bag or wrap them in newspaper. Put a card in the box, stating the date on which the fish were taken.

34

STILL WATER

You want to know about fishing in still water. Perhaps it is because you have heard of the great trout taken from the Scottish Lochs. In 1886 a trout weighing 39 lb. 8 oz. was caught in the famous Loch Awe. But such monsters are not to be taken on the fly. Spinning or trolling is the way of taking them, but we are fly-fishermen. Loch fishing in Scotland is there for the asking and much of it is free. There are one or two good lakes in Wales – Bala and Vyrnwy are really good, but they do not offer free fishing. In England we have to be content with reservoirs which normally belong to water boards or municipalities. Your fishing on these is usually obtained by way of the daily ticket which will probably cost you from ten shillings to as much as a pound. And before we go any farther, when you try your luck in a local reservoir be quite sure you know the rules and regulations. They are printed, usually, on the reverse side of the ticket, and they will state the size, the number of fish which may be taken, and so on. However, the possession of a daily ticket does not allow you to fish without a trout licence.

Still-water fly fishing is a chancy business. Blank days are fairly frequent, but you may be lucky enough to take a really good fish. The rod you have is not perhaps quite what is needed for still water, though you may make do with it. A 10-ft. rod is the thing! Your line will serve, and, of course, nylon for casts doesn't matter because it is so cheap. I'd use 3½ lb. breaking-strain cast point.

How to fish still water? That is the problem. Usually, unless the loch is small, fishing from the bank does not allow you any hope of covering much water. I have waded small lochs in the Hebrides and done quite well, but it is very risky and not to be attempted unless you have a friend with you. You should both know the water like the palms of your hands and you should both be strong swimmers. It is easy to put the wrong foot forward at the wrong time when wading, even when you can see the bottom.

The alternative is fishing from a boat. Fishing from a boat is forbidden on most of our reservoirs and on the free lochs there are no boats to be had. On those lochs where boats are available you must pay for the fishing and pay for the boat, plus a tip for the boatman at the end of the day. So it amounts to quite an expensive little bit of sport.

Still, you may be fortunate enough to be with a party who can afford to hire a boat and if two or three of you are casting from the same boat, be very careful. There is generally a wind, if only a light one, blowing across the water to add to the risk, and if one is the least bit careless someone stands a good chance of having a fly fixed in the face, or even worse, in the eye. I am not trying to put you off, far from it, but I must warn you of the dangers.

Here is the golden rule: whether in a boat, or fishing from the bank, fish only the lee shore. The reason for this is obvious. The wind blows the insect life to the lee shore and the trout are fully aware of that. And if you want to catch a really big one, fish close to the lee shore at evening time.

When there is no rise you must fish with the wet fly, and in loch fishing I think the use of three flies, a tail and two droppers, is reasonable.

But there is often a good hatch of fly on a loch, and then you should chance the dry fly. I do not know why, but there seems to be an odd idea that loch trout don't take kindly to dry fly. All I can say is – don't you believe it. A feeding fish in still water has his own little area – a yard or two either side of him. You may get him with the first cast, but if you don't, keep plugging away. Your fly will be just where it should be in a very little time.

On some lochs there are fine hatches of mayfly during the 'Duffers' Fortnight' and at this time there is a reasonable chance of taking a specimen fish. The blow-line is the best tackle to use, though it is so easy that there isn't much satisfaction in taking a specimen fish by this method.

Still-water fishing is, on the whole, much more profitable in the evening than in the day, and I have heard that on some water night fishing is even better. Unfortunately night fishing on reservoirs is often forbidden.

While I prefer to fish running water, I am not going to say that there is no thrill in fishing the still. There is always the possibility of catching a specimen fish so big that it lives in the angler's dreams, and there is the magic scenery of the lonely loch surrounded by purple mountains towering into the early night sky.

I once saw both ends of a rainbow when I was fishing Loch Langabhat in the Isle of Lewis. There was a sudden rainstorm followed by sunshine. Langabhat is a long loch, and when the rainbow came it stretched from one end of the loch to the other. It was like an enchanted bridge which shimmered against the blue and purple hues of the mountains. I thought of the crock of gold but I didn't know which end to look. However, I took some good fish that day. That rainbow has remained one of my pleasantest angling memories. If you go still-water fishing in the Scottish Highlands you may be lucky enough to take a char. The char is a member of the salmon family. They really belong to the icy tarns of the far north and no one knows how a few have found their way to the lochs. They will take the same flies as their cousins, the trout, and should you take one, you will see what a beautiful fish it is. Admire its gleaming colours but put it back. I once saw one taken and kept. Within minutes all its beauty had faded, and ever since then I have felt that keeping a char is something I'd rather not have on my angling conscience. The best advice I can give you about still-water fly fishing is to seek out the local anglers for the essential information on favourite flies and the little peculiarities of the water. And don't forget to be very careful when casting from a boat. You may get away with a moment's thoughtlessness but on the other hand it could end in maiming a friend for life. The price is too high to take unnecessary risks.

35

COARSE FISHING WITH THE FLY

Now let us consider those fish which are so neglected by the fly fisherman. I believe they are neglected because the advantages they offer at certain times are not generally realized.

Let us take July and August, two months which offer the trout fisherman little sport usually because the smaller streams are very low and too clear. A month of real summer weather, plenty of sun and no rain, plays havoc with the trout streams of the hills and moors. They become little more than mere trickles and quite hopeless for fishing.

During those bad times we can turn to the larger waters, rivers, canals and even ponds. In water where there are grayling, you may fish and do well for a month or so after the trout season has closed. (The season for trout is from March to the end of September, for coarse fish from the 16th June to the end of February.) I have known grayling to be taken on a fly as late as the end of November, though I must admit it was a particularly mild November.

Nevertheless, the advantages are there, and the keen and sensible angler should not fail to avail himself of them.

You will not require a licence for coarse fish as you do for game fish, but you will, of course, need permission to fish private water or to be a member of an angling club in order to fish club waters. But just as there are rules and regulations for trout fishing, so there are for coarse fishing and you must make yourself familiar with them. The trout tackle you have already will do admirably for coarse fish.

We have already discussed the appearance and characteristics of the grayling in the section on float fishing. Now we shall see how she takes the fly.

The methods to use for the grayling are wet fly, up or down-stream, and dry fly – just as you would for trout. And what flies? Once again it is all a matter of locality. The fly-fisherman must never forget that a fish is familiar only with the insect life its own particular water provides. While sometimes a fish can be tempted by a strange fly, normally they are apt to be suspicious of anything just a little bit unusual. However, I have found two flies, an Olive-dun and a Black Gnat, which seem to be welcomed on most water. To be on the safe side, though, I must advise you once more to talk to local anglers about it.

Having selected the flies, you go about your fishing just as you would for trout, except that grayling like the fast water, particularly when it flows over a gravel bottom where there are no weeds. Here is something worth-while to remember: when you have fished a fast run for grayling, you will be well advised to fish the deep water for trout, for when the grayling are taking in a run, there is a very good chance the trout will do the same in the deeper, slower water.

Now whether you are fishing wet, up or down, or dry, you will find the grayling often comes 'short' to the fly – just managing to miss it. The reason is that they lie deeper in the water than trout and consequently they rise up almost vertically, which gives them less time to judge distances than the trout lying nearer the surface. Therefore, when you rise the grayling and there is no contact, try again, and sooner or later the grayling will judge the correct distance and timing – the rest is up to you.

A grayling isn't so easily put off as a trout. You must obviously keep to the rules – in other words, don't let yourself be spotted or tread heavily – yet a bad cast, a bad strike which will scare a trout out of its wits won't bother the grayling one little bit. I have, on many occasions, actually pricked them and yet, next cast, back they came again.

If you are fishing with a wet fly, whether up or downstream, you must strike quickly; if you are fishing dry the strike must not be too quick. It is just the same as for the trout.

But when you are fast into a good one you will need all your skill. A grayling very seldom bores down into the depths, as does a trout; instead it shakes the line just as a dog shakes a rat. You cannot relax until you have her in the net and away from the water.

The chub or chavender will rise to the fly almost as eagerly as the grayling, but then the chub is a fish to which all food is rather more than welcome.

What flies to try? My own preference are Zulus, Black Gnats and Coch-y-Bonndu, but, as in all fly fishing, patterns vary with the locality. The chavender, as I prefer to call him, is a very strong fish, so if you are lucky enough to hook a big one you will need a fairly strong cast, round about 3 to 3½ lb. breaking-strain. His first dart for freedom when hooked is quite a thrill, but once you have foiled his first rush he gives in and comes to the net without a real kick in him. All the same, the chavender's first rush will test your skill.

Our chavender doesn't like mud and he doesn't like stagnant water either, so we must find a nice stretch, fairly deep and fairly strongly flowing. The big ones are only to be found in water that flows beneath trees, usually willows or elders. So choose a place where there are trees and shade and fast water flowing over gravel, to try the fly. Wet or dry? I do not think it is likely that you will take a big one on a dry fly. I think you should fish upstream with the wet fly. The chavender is not a bottom feeder, and he does not lie close to the surface as does a trout. If the water is 8 ft. deep the chavender will be lying almost 4 ft. down; half-way between the bottom and the surface. He likes to come up to take, and at that depth his cone of vision, or window, is quite extensive, so precious few tit-bits coming downstream pass unnoticed. Consequently the chavender very seldom rises in a swift rush; instead he comes up quite leisurely, takes, turns, and down he goes to his lie. And it is when he turns that you must strike. As you are fishing upstream and your fly will only be about an inch below the surface, you will see the 'shadow' or the gleam of the white belly, and if it is a good one – anything over 2 lb. – be ready.

You must remember that you are fishing beneath trees, and that trees have roots beneath the water surface which you cannot see, but the fish can. He knows where they are and he'll make a dash for them. Once he's there you can wish him goodbye. As the chavender turns and you strike put on side strain at once or you may be too late. If you succeed in turning the fish all well and good. He is as good as yours and half-way to the net. He may try another dash but it will be a half-hearted effort and after that he will just give in.

If you take a good chavender from a stretch or swim you will usually take another, but should the cast be broken or you lose your fish for some other reason it is better to seek another stretch. However the chavender takes the fly so deliberately that it would be rather difficult to fail to hook him on the strike.

I have already talked in detail about the brave little fighter, the dace, and if you want real sport with him I suggest that you fish very, very fine. Instead of using a nylon cast use one of horse-hair. You will need all your skill to take one of $\frac{1}{4}$ lb. on such a fine cast. Which flies to use? For dace I suggest Black Gnat or Blue Upright flies.

Dace play around in shoals in fast water so when you hook one get him away with as little disturbance as possible so that the other dace can be taken.

How best to try for them? You can try wet fly fishing up or downstream, but I prefer to fish for them dry. The dace is essentially a surface feeder so I think dry is the better way. As you are using a horse-hair cast you will have to be careful how you strike: it must be very fast but not too hard. It has to be fast for there is no fish in the water which can suck in a fly and blow it out more quickly than the dace.

You will miss dozens of rises at first, everyone does, but after a while you will be able to sense the timing and once that is done you will have good fun. It is also good practice at a time when trout fishing is out of the question.

I am often a little puzzled why it is that so very few of us ever try the roach with the fly. He will not take with the readiness of the grayling or the chavender, but take he will, and at a time when quite possibly the trout water is so low that it is unfishable.

Where to fish for him? Find a nice smooth stretch of water gently flowing between weed banks. The roach is a very obliging feeder. According to the state of the water he may feed from almost on the bottom to the surface. And in hot weather – which is when you will be after him – he will take fly on the surface.

You may fish wet or dry, but if wet I advise you to fish upstream. I *have* taken roach on a wet fly downstream, but I have done much better by fishing up.

Flies? I have looked up my records which go back very many years, and I see from them that when fishing with the fly for coarse fish I have accounted for the majority with a Black Gnat or a Zulu, which is a rather larger pattern of a Black Gnat with a tiny red tag. From those facts I have assumed that for some reason coarse fish look favourably upon black flies. I have taken them with various other patterns: Coch-y-Bonndu, Blue Upright, and very occasionally with Wickham's Fancy.

Cast between the weed banks. The roach is as shy as most fish so you must not take chances. He never appears to be in any hurry, therefore you do not strike too quickly. Fish fine with 1 lb. to 1½ lb. breaking-strain point, and because roach go about in shoals do your utmost to steer a hooked fish away from the others. A good roach, from ½ lb. to 1 lb. will give quite a fight on fine tackle, and a two-pounder (you will have to be lucky to hook one of that weight) a real battle!

Of course they are no good for the pan so you will return them to the water. In doing so, be extra careful about it because their rather large silver scales come away from the body very easily.

There is another way of having fun with the roach. Float fishermen do not trouble to take the roach in the heat of a summer day. Often when the sun is up you will see a shoal of roach basking on the surface. Most of them will be rather small, but here and there you will see a really good one. Keep well out of sight and, making no noise with your feet, get behind the shoal. Mark down the big ones and try to put a fly, dry of course, a few inches above their noses. They will probably ignore it at first. Yet, if you cast well and present the fly very gently, the fish will not be worried. After two or three times it is more than probable that the roach, either from curiosity or irritation, will take the fly.

Yes, roach can give you good fun when it is most needed, and I often wonder why fly-fishermen do not realize it.

Now let us discuss the rudd.

We should be grateful to the rudd for he is one of the very few fish which are ready to take on the hottest days of the two bad months of the year: July and August. Unfortunately rudd are not so easily found as roach.

There is one difference between roach and rudd which is of importance to the fly-fisherman. While the roach does at times feed on the bottom, the rudd never does. He is essentially a surface feeder, and consequently takes the fly more readily. You will find him in slow water where there is plenty of weed, and a good rudd will give you a fight, but you must fish fine.

I am inclined to think that it is better to keep to the dry fly for rudd. They are rather more shy than roach and it is better to approach them from behind. I suggest you try them in the same manner as you would the roach, but strike just a little faster as the rudd's rise is bolder, more hurried, otherwise you will probably miss him. On a hot summer day they bask in shoals. It takes a good deal of skill to cast for the big ones without scaring them and the smaller ones nearby.

Use the same flies as for the roach. You can't go wrong with a Black Gnat, though local anglers will have their own special favourites which suit the local conditions.

36

IN CONCLUSION

AND now we must come to the end of this book. There is nothing more for me to tell you.

I have tried to tell you, in a simple way, the first principles of fishing with the float and artificial fly. When you have mastered them you will be able to practise the gentlest of arts with every chance of success. I cannot turn you into an expert angler over night. Tuition will help, of course, but if you are to become truly expert – then it will be only by your own efforts. Practice, observation and a love of the sport are the answers.

But to be an expert and take fish when no one else is able to do so isn't the beginning or the end of angling. I have a friend who is a shocking angler. If there is the slightest chance of making a hash of things he will do so every time. He seldom takes a good fish but I know no one who loves his fishing more than he does. You see, he has the true angler's outlook He doesn't worry about taking fish. He simply loves fishing. He enjoys every moment of it – and that is what matters.

I should like you to become experts, but far rather would I like to see you enjoying yourselves. Anglers are some of the very few people who can get away from the worries of this modern world – the mad rushing here, there and everywhere for no sensible reason.

When the angler walks beside the water he finds himself at peace with the world.

He listens to the water laughing or sighing. He sees the green of small hedge-enclosed fields, flecked with daisies and buttercups; cattle, head to tail, seeking shade beneath oaks that were young when Izaak Walton angled and wrote of Anglers and the Honest

171

Men. Perhaps he sees the buzzard hawks hovering on apparently motionless wings in the blue sky of a June day, or hears the cawing of rooks against the bleating of sheep. He sees the deep pool ahead and dreams of the big one that he hopes to catch one day. He is one with his surroundings. The day will end and he will go back to his home, content in the knowledge that he can return to the magic of the waterside where his troubles will be soothed away.

I hope that my advice in this book has helped you towards the water where the fish will twitch the float or rise to the fly, and where there is peace for all who walk there.

Good luck go with you!

INDEX